Recipes and Stories from Ireland's
Wild Atlantic Way

ABOUT THE AUTHOR

Jody Eddy is a Minnesota native who graduated from the Institute of Culinary Education in Manhattan. She has cooked at Jean-Georges and Tabla in New York and Heston Blumenthal's The Fat Duck in Bray, England. She is the former executive editor of *Art Culinaire*, organises food conferences in the United States and India and leads culinary tours in Iceland and Cuba. Her first cookbook was nominated for a James Beard Award and her second won an IACP Judge's Choice Award. She writes for *Saveur*, *Travel + Leisure*, *The Wall Street Journal*, *The Guardian*, *Food & Wine*, *Food Arts*, *Plate* and *The Local Palate*. This is her third cookbook.

ABOUT THE PHOTOGRAPHER

Sandeep Patwal is a food and travel photographer based in Ireland. He has shot for *Saveur*, *Travel + Leisure*, *The Wall Street Journal*, *Food Arts*, *Plate*, *Food Republic* and *Zester Daily*, among others. His location along the Wild Atlantic Way in the heart of County Mayo makes him the ideal photographer to comprehensively capture the food, people and places along the route. For further information, visit www.sandeeppatwal.com.

Recipes and Stories from

Ireland's Wild Atlantic Way

Jody Eddy
Photography by Sandeep Patwal

Gill Books

Gill Books

Hume Avenue

Park West

Dublin 12

www.gillbooks.ie

Gill Books is an imprint of M.H. Gill & Co.

© Jody Eddy 2016

978 0717 1 6989 4

←————————→

Designed by Tanya M. Ross, elementinc.ie
Photography by Sandeep Patwal
Printed by Printer Trento Srl, Italy

All photographs supplied by Sandeep Patwal except the following:
© iStock.com / Kristina_CH, p26; © iStock.com / Kevin Alexander George, p127.

This book is typeset in Quicksand 8.5pt on 10pt.

The paper used in this book comes from the wood pulp of managed forests.
For every tree felled, at least one tree is planted, thereby renewing natural resources.

A CIP catalogue record for this book is available from the British Library.

5 4 3 2 1

This book is dedicated to my grandmother, Evelyn Bragelman, who grew up on a small family farm in rural Minnesota and was the first to inspire in me a love of locally sourced food and an abiding appreciation and respect for the people who produce it.

ACKNOWLEDGEMENTS

We would like to thank all of the extraordinary food producers, advocates and chefs we've had the good fortune to meet along the Wild Atlantic Way. We would also like to thank Amy Collins, Mary Eddy, Madhuri and Puran Singh, Anup and Kelitta Patwal, Kevin Thornton, Atul and Meenakshi Bisht, Raychel O'Keefe, Sheila Pearson, Peter Rosene, Mark Anderson, Colleen Foster, Bridget and Ari McGinty and John Mulcahy for all their unwavering support.

CONTENTS

CHAPTER 1

Seaweed, Prannie Rhatigan 1

Fresh Start Seaweed and Green Tea Smoothie 2

Beer-Battered Fried Cod Sandwiches with Lemon-Dulse Mayonnaise 3

Roasted Red Pepper Hummus with Dulse Pitta Chips 5

Garlic and Nettle Soup with Chive Yogurt 6

Seaweed Pesto Chicken Pasta 9

Seaweed Bathing and Farming 10

Donegal Travel Guide 13

CHAPTER 2

Shells Café and Little Shop, Jane and Myles Lamberth 15

Smoked Salmon and Grilled Asparagus Eggs Benedict with Mustard Hollandaise 16

Roasted Beetroot and Rosemary Salad 19

Chicken, Cabbage and Carrot Spring Rolls 20

Grilled Turkey and Smoked Cheddar Brown Bread Sandwiches with Thyme-Walnut
  Cream Cheese 22

Spiced Plum and Almond Tart with Cinnamon Crème Fraîche 23

Eithna's By the Sea 24

Sligo Travel Guide 27

CHAPTER 3

Achill Island Sea Salt, Kieran and Marjorie O'Malley 29

Roasted Parsnip Soup with Green Apples and Hazelnuts 30

Braised Juniper and Black Pepper Venison with Colcannon 31

Barbecue Pulled Pork and Pickled Radish Bap 33

Lazy Sunday Sausage and Spinach Rolls with Honey Mustard Sauce 34

Chocolate and Whiskey Flourless Cake with Blackberry Sauce and Sea Salt 36

Irish Honey 37

Mayo Travel Guide 39

CHAPTER 4

Achill Mountain Lamb, Martin Calvey and Family ———————————— 41

Lamb Burgers with Creamy Red Cabbage Slaw ———————————— 42

Summer Berry Dutch Baby ———————————————————————— 44

Sweet Potato, White Bean and Lamb Stew ———————————————— 45

Sloe Gin Fizz ———————————————————————————————— 47

Roast Beef and Vegetables with Port Gravy and Horseradish Cream ———— 48

Foraging ———————————————————————————————————— 49

Achill Island Travel Guide ——————————————————————— 51

CHAPTER 5

Marty's Mussels, Catherine and Marty Nee ——————————————— 53

Smoked Bacon and Mussel Chowder with Corn and Lemon Cream ———— 54

Renvyle Steamed Mussels ———————————————————————— 55

Baked White Fish with Black Olives and Roasted Tomato Sauce ———————— 56

Elderflower Bellini ———————————————————————————— 58

Seared Scallop and Sugar Snap Pea Linguine with Rocket and Brown Butter Sauce —— 60

Irish Soda Bread ——————————————————————————————— 61

Connemara Travel Guide ————————————————————————— 63

CHAPTER 6

Independent Brewing, Kevin O'Hara ————————————————————— 65

Rhubarb and Strawberry Muffins with Brown Sugar Glaze ————————— 66

Wild Game Terrine ———————————————————————————— 67

Beef, Stout and Wild Mushroom Pie ————————————————————— 68

Crispy Duck Breasts with Caramelised Celeriac and Red Onion Jam ———— 70

Chocolate Stout and Sea Salt Ice Cream ——————————————————— 72

Irish Cider ——————————————————————————————————— 73

Galway Travel Guide ——————————————————————————— 75

CHAPTER 7

Aran Island Goats' Cheese (Cáis Gabhair Arann), Gabriel Faherty —————— 77

Sundried Tomato and Goat's Cheese Scones ———————————————— 78

Lickety-Split Homemade Cheese ——————————————————————— 79

Black Pudding and Goat's Cheese Frittata _____ 80

Toasted Hazelnut Pizza with Roasted Pears, Bacon and Goat's Cheese _____ 83

Roasted Cauliflower and Goat's Cheese Risotto _____ 84

Irish Butter _____ 85

Inishmore Travel Guide _____ 87

CHAPTER 8

Kelly Oysters, Michael Kelly and Family _____ 89

Spiced Pumpkin Biscuits with Honey Butter _____ 90

Galway Mule _____ 91

Oyster Fritters with Caper Dipping Sauce _____ 92

Panko-Crusted Crab Cakes with Blackened Tomato Salsa _____ 95

Roasted Oysters with Horseradish Remoulade and Shallot Mignonette _____ 96

A Brief History of the Irish Oyster _____ 97

Kerry Travel Guide _____ 99

CHAPTER 9

Hazel Mountain Chocolate, John and Kasha Connolly _____ 101

Smoked Trout and Barley Salad with Lime Vinaigrette _____ 102

Rosehip Syrup _____ 105

Double Chocolate and Toasted Oat Cookies _____ 107

Irish Soda Bread _____ 108

Chocolate Poitín Old Fashioned _____ 109

Rigney's Farm _____ 110

Clare Travel Guide _____ 113

CHAPTER 10

Gubbeen Farm, Fingal Ferguson and Family _____ 115

West Cork Porridge with Maple Syrup and Toasted Pecans _____ 116

Smoked Salmon Dip _____ 117

Grilled Prawn and Smoked Sausage Salad with Pickled Lemon Cucumbers _____ 118

Slow-Roasted Pork Tenderloin with Lentils and Kale _____ 121

Home Kitchen Dingle Clam Bake _____ 122

Fish Smoking _____ 123

Cork Travel Guide _____ 125

FOR MILLENNIA, SEAWEED WAS INDISPENSABLE IN IRELAND'S CULINARY REPERTOIRE, ESSENTIAL TO THE HEALTH OF IRISH FIELDS AND EVEN A WELCOME ADDITION TO IRISH BATHTUBS.

1 | Seaweed

Prannie Rhatigan

Prannie Rhatigan is on a quest to remind the Irish people of a tradition once integral to the welfare and well-being of their ancestors. For millennia, seaweed was indispensable in this nation's culinary repertoire, essential to the health of Irish fields and even a welcome addition to Irish bathtubs. It was appreciated for its texture and briny flavour in recipes and its abundance of healthful nutrients and minerals, for the wonders it worked as a fertiliser in the garden and for its rejuvenating properties when added to the bathtub.

The modern world has little time for seaweed's virtues and its veneration has waned with the encroachment of new technology and a faster pace of life, but Prannie, a medical doctor and author of the book *The Irish Seaweed Kitchen*, is on a one-woman mission to remind her nation of the time not so long ago when seaweed was a fundamental part of the cook and gardener's repertoire.

Prannie leads seaweed identification walks along the Streedagh coast near the surfing village of Strandhill in north-western Ireland and is renowned as a seaweed expert throughout the world. As she investigates a few of Ireland's over 600 seaweed varieties strewn across the wet sand along her seaweed walk, she reminisces, 'As children, we would harvest seaweed along the shoreline with my father, who always believed in seaweed's ability to heal and maintain optimal health. If people saw us doing it, they would say, "Pity, you've hit upon hard times", because for so long, harvesting seaweed meant that you had run low on your resources and needed to collect it to get by. They have forgotten how valued seaweed used to be to the Irish people. I am trying to help them remember.'

Prannie and a growing number of others are working to liberate seaweed from the association with destitution that arose during times of hardship by introducing it once more into their kitchens, bathtubs and gardens. The seaweed pioneer, whose blue eyes gleam with a vitality derived from a lifetime of seaweed consumption, says, 'Today there is a renewed curiosity and appreciation for seaweed in Ireland and I find fulfilment in teaching my fellow countrymen about a tradition that is fundamental to who we are as Irish people.'

FRESH START SEAWEED AND GREEN TEA SMOOTHIE

Prannie Rhatigan's lovely cookbook, *The Irish Seaweed Kitchen,* features her 'Addictive Green Smoothie' recipe comprised of seaweed and other uplifting ingredients to ensure an energising start to the day. This smoothie is inspired by Prannie's recipe, delivering the same effervescent boost we sometimes need to enliven an early morning. Ingredients such as linseeds and chia seeds might be challenging to source, so they are only a suggestion for an additional nutritional boost. If you are more of a juice person than a tea person, substitute your favourite fruit or vegetable juice for the green tea.

There are countless ways to alter the flavour and health benefits of this smoothie by modifying its ingredients based upon the season or the goodies available at the market, but the one mainstay should be the seaweed since it's the element that will always guarantee a nourishing start to the day. The company Wild Irish Sea Veg has a wide array of seaweed products, including several milled varieties of seaweed that are perfect to not only add to this smoothie but to sprinkle over everything from salads to soups to baked fish. Nori makes a nice seaweed substitute should you have trouble sourcing the dulse and carrageen suggested in this recipe.

SERVES 1
PREPARATION TIME: 10 MINUTES

1 pear, cored and roughly chopped
1 banana, thickly sliced
1 plum, stoned and roughly chopped
1 handful blueberries
1 handful torn kale or spinach leaves
1 tsp linseeds
1 tsp milled chia seeds
1 tbsp milled dulse
1 tbsp milled carrageen
1 tbsp pumpkin seeds
6 almonds
1 tbsp honey
240 ml coconut water
240 ml green tea (retain the tea bag and
    also add the leaves themselves to your
    smoothie)

Place all of the ingredients in a blender. Beginning at a low speed, blend until just incorporated and then increase the speed to the highest setting and blend until smooth. Pour into a glass and enjoy.

BEER-BATTERED FRIED COD SANDWICHES WITH LEMON-DULSE MAYONNAISE

Beer-battered cod is a crowd favourite in the Sligo area where Prannie Rhatigan harvests her seaweed. In this recipe, dulse is incorporated into both the mayonnaise and the batter to transport you to the Irish shore, where nothing tastes better on a sunny afternoon than a fried fish sandwich and an ice-cold pint. Buying milled seaweed makes it easy to incorporate it into your favourite dipping sauce, batter, soup or salad. Use it as a sprinkle in the same way you would add salt or pepper to a dish.

SERVES 4
PREPARATION TIME: 30 MINUTES

For the lemon-dulse mayonnaise:
1 tbsp freshly squeezed lemon juice
2 tbsp capers, finely chopped
2 tsp milled dulse
200 g mayonnaise
salt, to taste

For the beer-battered cod sandwiches:
125 g plain flour
1 tsp chilli flakes
2 tsp milled dulse
180 ml light beer, such as a lager, pale ale
   or an IPA
60 ml cold water
1 egg yolk
vegetable oil, as needed
4 x 200 g skinless, boneless cod fillets
salt and freshly ground black pepper, to
   taste

To serve:
4 burger buns or baps
Cheddar cheese, grated
1 tomato, sliced in rings
handful rocket
1 red onion, sliced in rings

To make the lemon-dulse mayonnaise, whisk together the lemon juice, capers, dulse and mayonnaise in a bowl. Season with salt and refrigerate until chilled.

Next, place the flour, chilli flakes and dulse in a large bowl and stir to combine. In a second bowl, add the beer, cold water and egg yolk and whisk until smooth. Add the liquid to the flour and whisk until the batter just comes together and is still a bit lumpy.

Heat the oil in a large frying pan until gently bubbling and place a rack lined with kitchen paper over a baking tray. Season the fish fillets on both sides with salt and pepper and dip in the batter until completely covered. Fry in the oil until golden brown, for about three minutes per side. Remove from the oil using a metal spatula and transfer to the kitchen paper. Season with salt.

Preheat the oven to 180°C and toast the buns, sliced side up, until the edges start to turn golden brown. Sprinkle with cheese and continue to toast until melted, for about one minute. Spread the bun bottoms with a generous layer of mayonnaise and top with a fried fillet, tomato, rocket and red onion. Serve with a side of lemon wedges while the fish is still nice and hot.

ROASTED RED PEPPER HUMMUS WITH DULSE PITTA CHIPS

This is a fun way to add a little seaweed spark to a standard hummus recipe. Feel free to substitute yellow or orange peppers or, if you're in a time pinch, use a small jar of roasted peppers instead. If you want to store your peppers before using them, toss them with a little olive oil and keep in the refrigerator in a covered container for up to two weeks. The dulse chips perk up boring pitta, giving them a briny hint of flavour and pop of colour.

SERVES 4
PREPARATION TIME: 30 MINUTES

For the roasted red pepper hummus:
4 red peppers
400 g chickpeas
1 clove garlic, minced
1 tbsp freshly squeezed lemon juice, plus additional for seasoning
1 tsp cumin seeds, toasted
pinch of chilli flakes, optional
1 tbsp olive oil, plus additional as necessary
salt and freshly ground black pepper, to taste

For the dulse pitta chips:
4 round pitta, cut into triangles
olive oil, for brushing
milled dulse, as needed
salt, as needed

To serve:
lemon wedges

Preheat the oven to 190°C. Place the peppers on a baking tray and roast in the oven until the skin is completely charred, for about 35 minutes. Turn twice during the process for even charring. Using tongs, place the peppers in a bowl and cover securely with cling film. Alternatively, use tin foil or place the peppers in zippable sandwich bags. Set aside at room temperature until the peppers are cool enough to handle. Remove the stems and slice the peppers in quarters. Using your fingers, remove the seeds and the skin and discard.

Transfer the peppers to a food processor along with the rest of the ingredients except the oil and salt. Pulse until incorporated while adding enough oil to create a smooth but thick consistency, about one tablespoon. Be careful not to over-process the hummus or it could become runny. Season with salt, along with additional lemon juice, if desired.

While the peppers cool, reduce the oven temperature to 180°C. Place the pitta triangles on a baking tray and brush with oil. Sprinkle with dulse and season with salt. Bake until the pitta chips begin to turn golden brown along the edges. Remove from the oven and cool to room temperature. Serve the hummus with the pitta chips and lemon wedges.

GARLIC AND NETTLE SOUP WITH CHIVE YOGURT

Nettles really do sting! But if handled properly and harvested at the right time, their many virtues far outweigh their prickliness. Nettle-picking, like seaweed-harvesting, is an Irish culinary tradition now being rediscovered due to nettles' flavour, nutritional benefits and widespread availability in hedgegrows across the Wild Atlantic Way. The best time to use nettles' wonderful little leaves, which are rich in iron and vitamin C, is in early spring when their stingers are young and not potent but their flavour is sweet and robust. The trick is to use only the small leaves near the top of the plant and to wear rubber gloves during the harvesting and preparation process. Once they've been blanched, they're benign, nutritious and flavourful. Use them in any dish that calls for spinach or, as the Irish used to do (and some still do), to create a spring tonic that is prescribed three times during the season to ward off arthritis and increase blood circulation. Nettles are sometimes applied to burns and the ancient Romans used to consume nettles for its diuretic properties.

The Irish used to use the fibrous leaves to weave cloth bags and nets, fed wilted nettles to their livestock and diluted nettles in water for a robust fertiliser in the fields. It was once believed that a patch of nettles indicated where the faeries lived and even their sting was honoured as protection from witchcraft and dark magic. Considering nettles' powerful nutritional benefits, you might as well make this soup, which is thickened with potatoes and enriched with butter and chicken stock, to ward off sorcerous spells while keeping yourself healthy at the same time.

SERVES 4
PREPARATION TIME: 35 MINUTES

For the garlic and nettle soup:
½ carrier bag of young nettle tops (wear rubber gloves when harvesting and handling)
30 g butter
1 medium onion, roughly chopped
2 cloves garlic, roughly chopped
4 large Rooster or white potatoes, peeled and roughly chopped
1 celery stalk, roughly chopped
1 litre chicken or vegetable stock
2 bay leaves
4 sprigs thyme
1 tbsp freshly squeezed lemon juice, plus additional for seasoning
salt and freshly ground black pepper, to taste

For the chive yogurt:
100 g yogurt
chives, roughly chopped
salt, to taste

Bring a saucepan of salted water to a boil and prepare an ice bath. Wearing rubber gloves, place the nettles in the boiling water and simmer for two minutes. Using tongs or a slotted spoon, transfer the nettles to the ice bath in order to shock them and prevent discolouration. Melt the butter in a sauté pan and sauté the onions and garlic until the onions are translucent and the garlic is aromatic.

Add the potatoes and celery and sauté for a few minutes more. Add the stock, bay leaves, thyme springs and lemon juice and bring to a boil. Reduce the heat, add the nettles and gently simmer until the potatoes are tender, for about 10 minutes.

Meanwhile, whisk together the yogurt and chives with a little water for a slightly runny consistency. Season with salt.

Using tongs, remove the bay and the thyme from the pan and transfer the soup to a blender. Using caution to prevent splattering, blend at the lowest speed until incorporated, then increase the speed to its highest setting and purée until smooth. Season with salt and pepper and additional lemon juice, if desired. To serve, spoon the soup into a bowl, drizzle with the yogurt and garnish with chives.

SEAWEED PESTO CHICKEN PASTA

Milled seaweed is easily tucked into this garlicky pesto recipe, infusing it with a subtle saline flavour that pairs well with the lush notes of basil and lemony parsley. Kelp, which is rich in vitamin A, calcium and amino acids, is used in this recipe, but any seaweed variety, such as bladderwrack or dulse, would work well too. Substitute hazelnuts for the almonds for an earthier flavour or walnuts for a more delicate taste. The pesto will keep in a covered container in the refrigerator for up to one week and is also fantastic as a sandwich spread or to gussy up scrambled eggs.

SERVES 4
PREPARATION TIME: 30 MINUTES

For the seaweed pesto:
2 large bunches basil (including stems)
6 sprigs parsley (including stems)
150 g almonds, toasted
4 cloves garlic
150 g Parmesan cheese, grated
1 tbsp milled kelp
8 tbsp olive oil
salt and freshly ground black pepper, to taste

For the chicken pasta:
500 g fusilli (or pasta of your choice)
1 tbsp olive oil
1 large red onion, roughly chopped
2 dried red chillies, rehydrated and finely chopped
2 skinless chicken breasts, cut into bite-size pieces
12 cherry tomatoes, halved

To serve:
almonds, roughly chopped and toasted
milled kelp

Combine the basil, parsley, almonds, garlic, Parmesan and kelp in a food processor and pulse while adding the olive oil in a slow, steady stream until the pesto is slightly smooth but still retains a little chunkiness. Season with salt and pepper.

Bring a saucepan of salted water to a boil. Add the pasta and simmer until just cooked through, for about eight minutes. Drain, return to the saucepan and cover to keep warm.

Heat one tablespoon of olive oil in a sauté pan and sauté the onion, chillies and chicken over a medium-high heat until the onion is translucent and the chicken is cooked through, for about nine minutes. Toss together the chicken, pesto and tomatoes with the pasta until well incorporated. Spoon into a bowl, garnish with chopped toasted almonds and sprinkle with kelp.

Seaweed Bathing and Farming

Mick Walton, a retired engineer in Strandhill, grows five-foot-long parsnips. No, he's not assisted by aliens and he doesn't concoct a magic potion in his underground laboratory. Instead, he relies upon the fortifying powers of Irish seaweed. Mick, an energetic man with a wisp of white hair and a fondness for ice cream cones, has always been an avid gardener. The introduction of seaweed to his soil dramatically changed the growing game for him. It all started when his son, Neil Walton, started VOYA Seaweed Baths.

Neil grew up long-distance running with his father. It was a passion that eventually led him to Australia to train as a professional triathlete. It was here that Neil discovered seaweed's ability to heal his aching body following his endurance workouts. Seaweed's ability to leach toxins from his aching muscles, minimise the fluids that accumulated in his body and replenish his system with rejuvenating minerals inspired Neil to open VOYA upon his return to Ireland in order to introduce his fellow countrymen to seaweed's virtues.

Ireland has a longstanding seaweed bath tradition. It's a practice stretching back all the way to Roman times and at the start of the twentieth century there were over 300 public seaweed baths speckled throughout the nation. Very few of these have survived but Neil did not let this deter him. He was determined to open the doors to VOYA in his hometown of Strandhill, where the remnants of the town's last seaweed bath, destroyed by a hurricane in the 1960s, still stands as a testament to Ireland's seaweed bathing legacy.

Neil's undertaking paid off and today VOYA is wildly successful, with a line of seaweed-based beauty products that are sold throughout the world. But with sustainability in mind, Neil needed to find a use for the seaweed he used in his bathtubs, which are filled with ocean water pumped from the shore. That's when Mick, his engineering mind programmed to find solutions, suggested he use it in his garden. This not only resulted in vegetables so large they boggle the mind, but also in the return of a tradition once embraced in this region: seaweed farming.

Mick, who also harvests the seaweed for VOYA, uses what he needs from the spa's seaweed surplus and then takes the rest to a community plot that anyone can access to fertilise their own farms and gardens. Farmers up and down the coast of western Ireland recall a time not so long ago when seaweed was pulled in from the sea to dry upon their fields before being tilled into the soil. It's a dying practice that was once integral to the vitality of Ireland's fields. The Waltons are rightfully proud of the contribution they have made to restoring the legacy of seaweed farming and bathing in Ireland. With every bath enjoyed and every vegetable grown in seaweed, Ireland comes one step closer to fortifying two hallowed rituals that will hopefully endure for generations to come.

WITH EVERY BATH
ENJOYED AND EVERY
VEGETABLE GROWN
IN SEAWEED, IRELAND
COMES ONE STEP
CLOSER TO FORTIFYING
TWO HALLOWED
RITUALS THAT WILL
HOPEFULLY ENDURE FOR
GENERATIONS TO COME.

> **"** Yet dearer still that Irish hill than all
> the world beside;
> It's home, sweet home, where'er I
> roam through lands and waters wide. **"**
>
> WILLIAM ALLINGHAM

Donegal
TRAVEL GUIDE

Just north of Sligo is County Donegal, where the Wild Atlantic Way begins along its wild tumble of cliffs and expansive beaches. The gateway to the county is Donegal Town, full of artisan butchers, lively pubs and inviting shops that encourage lingering long after the doors to Donegal Castle have closed to tourists each day. Along the way to Donegal from Sligo is Donegal Brewing Company in Ballyshannon, Ireland's oldest town. North of Donegal Town is stunning Lough Eske, with its elegant castle where visitors can stay for a night in the shadow of the silvery Blue Stack Mountains. The Slieve League cliffs near Carrick in south-western Donegal, the highest seaside cliffs in Europe, entice adventurous hikers to wander along their windswept precipices.

Further north is Letterkenny, the county's largest urban centre. A few miles from Letterkenny are Newmills Corn and Flax Mills, an operational mill featuring one of Ireland's largest waterwheels. Its oldest building dates back over four centuries and it's worth a visit to glimpse a scene from yesterday that has managed to remain just as vital and productive today. The Glenevin Waterfall isn't far away and Grianán of Aileach, a ring fort from the seventh century that was a royal site of Gaelic kings, should not be missed.

Tiny but visit-worthy, Inch Island in Lough Swilly, which is connected to the mainland by a bridge, is a birdwatcher's feast, especially in autumn when the swans return in impressive numbers from their breeding grounds in Iceland. Further west is must-see Glenveagh National Park and Castle, a paradise of forests, mountains, glens and lakes spilling out over thousands of hectares. A wander through the meticulously maintained Victorian gardens of the nineteenth-century fairy-tale Glenveagh Castle is as fortifying as the tea and scones waiting to be enjoyed at its charming tearoom.

After a visit to Inishowen Peninsula to wander the blustery beaches of Malin Head, Ireland's most northerly point, enjoy a pint at Kinnegar Brewing, a craft brewery on the western shores of Drongawn Lough, before stopping by Haven Smokehouse at the northern tip of Donegal. It is here that Sue Cruse and Declan McConnellogue swapped their frenetic existence in London for a life in Donegal, opening a traditional fish smokehouse where they smoke their salmon using turf in the same way that Declan's ancestors did for centuries.

BIG PLATES (FROM 12PM)

THE HOUSE BURGER	9.95
Big & Beefy & delicious with fresh cut chips & our home made tomato relish.	
Add Cheese or Bacon	1.50
THE SMOKEY BURGER	12.95
Beef burger topped with maple smoked cheese, dry cured bacon	
ULTIMATE BURGER	12.95
Still big & beefy, topped with fried banana, bacon and shells red onion marmalade. Served with fresh rocket and fresh cut chips	
CHICKEN BURGER	9.95
Butterfly fillet, topped with Irish Cheddar, basil mayo, tom, lettuce. Served with fresh cut chips	
CHICKPEA VEGGIE BURGER	10.95
Topped with balsamic cheese, roasted red peppers and homemade tomato relish with fresh cut chips	
PRAWN & CHORIZO PLATE	11.95
Pan fried king prawns with Gubeen Chorizo and crispy potato with salsa verde mayonaise. Delish!	
HOT POT OF THE DAY	
it's hot and it's served in a pot! Stewy goodness to warm the heart and belly served with a thick slice of fresh bread to mop up the deliciousness	
FISH AND CHIPS	9.95
Sustainable farmed white fish (haddock) giving the juno cod a break. Served simply in crispy batter with fresh cut chips & home mayonaise.	
SPECIAL OF THE DAY	
Check out our specials board for seasonal creative flair from our chefs	

SIDES	
CHIPS	3.00
SIDE SALAD	3.00
BROWN SODA BREAD	1.50
MARINATED TOMATOES	2.50

BIG & SMALL PLATES .05

THERE'S NO BETTER
PLACE TO FIND
SUSTENANCE AFTER
A BLUSTERY DAY OF
SURFING THAN SHELLS
CAFÉ, WHERE THE
BAKERY OVERFLOWS
WITH HOMEMADE
BROWN BREAD AND
HAZELNUT SCONES.

2 | Shells Café and Little Shop

Jane and Myles Lamberth

Myles Lamberth, a native of Cape Town, South Africa, met Jane Chambers, a former business and marketing professional from Dublin, after they both opted to trade in their former lives to surf the waves of Cornwall while figuring out what to do in their futures. It was a serendipitous encounter that eventually led them to marriage, cookbooks, children and a little place called Shells Café and Little Shop in the surfing community of Strandhill, County Sligo.

Myles always loved to cook, learning his trade while working as a safari and river guide in South Africa. It was in the twilight hours as he prepared meals over bonfires for his guests after a rough-and-tumble day of guiding that he realised he wanted to make his living as a cook. Now he just needed to sort out where he wanted to do it. After years of cooking in far-flung places around the world and operating ski chalets in the United States and Europe, he arrived in Cornwall, met Jane and the rest is Shells history.

The Lamberths' mirthful spirits and zest for living is mirrored in the welcoming environment of Shells Café, where the couple promote local ingredients on their menu, and in their Little Shop, which sells goodies from Irish food artisans such as Mill Lane Honey, Richmount Elderflower Cordial and Toons Bridge Dairy Buffalo Mozzarella along with their own *Surf Café Cookbook*.

Visitors can linger on the breezy deck, which overlooks a sprawling beach that catches ocean waves that surfers from around the world come to ride, and there's no better place to find sustenance after a blustery day of surfing than Shells Café, where the bakery overflows with loaves of homemade bread, hazelnut scones and cupcakes worthy of a Paris bakery window display. But this is north-western Ireland and the Lamberths have no time for pretension or artifice. Jane, with her sunny blonde curls and easy smile, and Myles, with his full beard and amiable nature, exude the kind of genuine hospitality that entices their guests to linger from the early morning over an apple chutney breakfast bap washed down by a hot cup of potent Fair Trade coffee to late afternoon after filling up on a hearty bowl of courgette and almond soup. The food at Shells Café is as fortifying as the company, with the Lamberths' embrace and promotion of local food producers further enhancing its infectious appeal.

SMOKED SALMON AND GRILLED ASPARAGUS EGGS BENEDICT WITH MUSTARD HOLLANDAISE

Shells Café in Strandhill serves an eggs benedict that shouldn't be passed up, no matter what time of day it is. Nothing quite compares to watching the surfers play in the rolling ocean waves of western Ireland while enjoying a hot cup of Shells coffee and their smoked salmon benedict. This recipe was inspired by that dish and while it might not be accompanied by the ocean mist to your face in the same way it is at Shells, it's tasty nonetheless. Don't let the hollandaise intimidate you. The only trick is to work quickly but with a gentle hand while adding in the butter. Once your sauce emulsifies you're well on your way to eggs benedict perfection.

SERVES 2
PREPARATION TIME: 35 MINUTES

For the asparagus:
6 asparagus spears
olive oil, as needed
salt and freshly ground black pepper, to
   taste

For the mustard hollandaise:
125 g butter
2 eggs, beaten
1 tsp wholegrain mustard
zest of ½ lemon
water, as needed
apple cider vinegar, as needed
salt and freshly ground black pepper, to
   taste

For the poached eggs:
2 tsp white wine vinegar
2 eggs
salt and freshly ground black pepper, to
   taste

To serve:
2 English muffins
4 slices smoked salmon
freshly grated nutmeg
sea salt

Preheat the oven to 180°C. Toss the asparagus with the oil, season with salt and pepper and arrange on a tin foil-lined baking tray. Roast until the edges begin to turn golden brown, for about six minutes.

To make the hollandaise, melt the butter in a small saucepan. Place two eggs in a heatproof bowl and place it over a saucepan of gently simmering water. Whisk in the mustard and lemon zest. Once incorporated, drizzle in the melted butter while whisking steadily but gently in order to avoid separating the sauce. Once it is emulsified, remove it from the heat; break it up by whisking in a few drops of water if it seizes up. Whisk in a little apple cider vinegar along with some salt and pepper to season. Cover it to keep it warm until you're ready to plate up the dish.

To make the poached eggs, bring a saucepan of water to a steady simmer. Add a dash of vinegar, which will help the eggs set faster. Break each egg into its own small ramekin or dish. Using a wooden spoon, create a calm little whirlpool in the pan before tipping the two eggs into it. The swirl will help the white wrap itself around the yolk as it poaches. Line a plate with kitchen paper. Cook the eggs for three minutes, then carefully remove with a slotted spoon and drain on the kitchen paper. Season with salt and pepper.

Toast the muffins as the eggs poach. To serve, place a muffin bottom on a plate and top with two slices of the smoked salmon and half of the roasted asparagus. Carefully transfer the poached egg on top of the asparagus and drizzle with a generous spoonful of hollandaise. Sprinkle with grated nutmeg and sea salt and enjoy.

ROASTED BEETROOT AND ROSEMARY SALAD

Shells Café serves a variety of fresh and seasonal salads each day, and in the colder months, beetroot features frequently. Beetroot, with its heartiness, nutritional assets and long shelf life, is a mainstay of the Irish winter diet. These garnet orbs, with their luscious flavour and velvety texture, are sometimes ostracised by home cooks who prefer a clean kitchen above the streaks of carmine juices beetroot tends to leave behind. One way to avoid the mess is to peel and chop the beetroot before it is cooked, like in this recipe. Pair them with a handful of toasted pumpkin seeds and the saltiness of feta and you've got yourself a perky salad to brighten this chilliest of winter days.

SERVES 4
PREPARATION TIME: 45 MINUTES

4 large red beetroots
leaves from 1 sprig rosemary, finely
    chopped
3 tbsp olive oil
salt and freshly ground black pepper, to
    taste

To serve:
pumpkin seeds, toasted
feta, crumbled
sea salt

Preheat the oven to 200°C. Peel each beetroot with a vegetable peeler and cut into bite-size pieces. Toss the beetroot together with the rosemary, olive oil and salt and pepper and arrange on a tin foil-lined baking tray. Roast until the beetroot is tender, for about 40 minutes.

To serve, arrange on a plate sprinkled with toasted pumpkin seeds, crumbled feta and sea salt.

CHICKEN, CABBAGE AND CARROT SPRING ROLLS

Carrots and cabbage are favourite Irish ingredients, but sometimes a day calls for a little more than a main with a side of steamed veg. Here these two beloved staples are incorporated into spring rolls that are lightly fried and ready to become your new favourite go-to appetiser. Cutting the veg as opposed to grating it might seem a bit laborious, but this cuts down on the liquid, which helps avoid a soggy roll. Try pork, beef or even crab or shrimp with a little cream cheese instead of chicken. Mixing up soy sauce with a pinch of ground ginger is a great dipping sauce to pair with the sweet and sour sauce or to replace it altogether. Avoid the temptation to overstuff, which can result in a burst roll when frying, and feel free to make these ahead of time. They freeze well so make an extra-large batch and fry them up whenever an afternoon at home calls for something a little festive.

MAKES 16 SPRING ROLLS
PREPARATION TIME: 25 MINUTES

2 tbsp sesame oil
2 chicken breasts, cut into cubes approx.
   1 cm x 1 cm
1 tsp finely chopped ginger
pinch of salt
2 large carrots, peeled, cut into 12 cm
   segments and sliced lengthwise into thin
   strips
½ head green cabbage, thinly sliced
4 spring onions, thinly sliced
1 clove garlic, finely chopped
2 tbsp oyster sauce
1 tbsp soy sauce
1 tbsp cornflour
1 tbsp cold water
16 spring roll wrappers
vegetable oil, as needed

To serve:
sweet and sour dipping sauce
soy sauce with a pinch of ground
   ginger

In a wok or a sauté pan, heat one tablespoon of sesame oil and sauté the chicken and ginger until the chicken is cooked through and the ginger is aromatic. Season with salt and transfer to a bowl and set aside. Heat the remaining sesame oil and sauté the carrots, cabbage, spring onions and garlic until the carrots are tender and the garlic is aromatic. Remove the pan from the heat and add the chicken and oyster and soy sauces. Transfer the filling in a uniform layer to a baking tray and cool to room temperature. Don't skip this step or the filling will make the wrappers soggy during the stuffing process.

Whisk together the cornflour and cold water and set aside. Remove the spring roll wrappers from the package and cover them with damp kitchen paper so they don't dry out. Keep the wrappers you're not using under the kitchen paper as you work. Lay a wrapper on a clean, dry work surface so that it looks like a diamond in front of you.

Spoon two tablespoons of the filling near the bottom corner and fold the bottom corner over it. Fold over one side, then the other and then roll up to form a roll. Before folding the top corner over the roll, wet with a little dab of the cornflour mix to encourage sealing. Try to avoid the formation of air pockets while rolling to prevent bubbles from forming during the frying process. Repeat with the remaining stuffing and wrappers. Once they have all been rolled, place them sealed side down on a baking tray and cover with damp kitchen paper.

Pour about 12 cm of vegetable oil into a wok or sauté pan until hot enough to form bubbles around the end of a wooden spoon when dipped into it. Transfer a few of the spring rolls to the oil using a slotted spoon. Be sure not to overcrowd them or they won't brown up properly. Fry until just golden brown, turning once during the process, about two minutes per side. They will continue to cook once removed from the oil so be sure to watch them carefully and remove just as they are turning brown. Drain on a kitchen paper-lined plate. Repeat with the remaining rolls.

Serve with sweet and sour dipping sauce along with a bowl of ginger-soy sauce.

GRILLED TURKEY AND SMOKED CHEDDAR BROWN BREAD SANDWICHES WITH THYME-WALNUT CREAM CHEESE

Shells Café has perfected the art of the sandwich with the same mastery that the Irish apply to making brown bread. Moist, slightly sweet slices are presented on restaurant and home tables throughout the nation as the ideal vehicle for slathering on a thick, creamy slab of Irish butter. In this recipe, they are spread with a layer of thyme-walnut cream cheese, which pairs so well with the smokiness of the smoked Cheddar cheese and mellow flavour of the turkey. Substitute your favourite smoked cheese for the Cheddar and chicken for the turkey if they're more to your liking. The green apples brighten up the sandwich and give it a little crunch while the cress provides a peppery after-note that could also be discovered in a handful of rocket. After the holidays, when every Irish household is trying to figure out what to do with their leftover Christmas turkey, this is a lovely way to gussy it up and make it seem brand new and exciting all over again.

SERVES 4
PREPARATION TIME: 20 MINUTES

For the thyme-walnut cream cheese:
150 g cream cheese, softened
50 g walnuts, toasted
leaves from 1 sprig thyme

For the brown bread sandwiches:
8 slices thick-cut turkey breast
smoked Cheddar cheese, sliced, as
  needed
8 slices brown bread
watercress, as needed
1 green apple, sliced and sprinkled with
  lemon juice to prevent browning

Place the cream cheese, walnuts and thyme in a bowl and stir vigorously until the cream cheese is slightly whipped.

Heat a sauté pan over a medium-high heat. Grill the turkey slices on the dry pan until heated through and golden brown on both sides.

Spread the cream cheese over a slice of brown bread and top with a slice of cheese, two slices of turkey, a handful of watercress and a few apple slices. Top with the second slice of bread, slice diagonally and serve.

SPICED PLUM AND ALMOND TART WITH CINNAMON CRÈME FRAÎCHE

Plums illuminate summer farmers' markets throughout Ireland. Here they are transformed into a tempting tart that will leave a wonderful aroma of cinnamon and cloves filling the room. The texture resembles a crumble and one of the only requirements for this forgiving dessert is to be sure to use chilled butter when preparing your base. This will ensure an appealing flakiness that works so well with the velvety attributes of the plums. You could substitute ice cream for the crème fraîche and feel free to omit the cloves if you're looking for a more subtle flavour.

MAKES 1 x 25 CM TART
PREPARATION TIME: 1 HOUR

For the cinnamon crème fraîche:
240 ml crème fraîche
1 tsp cinnamon

For the spiced plum and almond tart:
225 g plain flour
1 tsp baking powder
150 g almonds, finely chopped
175 g butter, chilled and cut into 2 cm
  cubes
1 egg yolk
pinch of salt
10 firm plums, seeded and cut into
  eighths
zest of ½ lime
1 tsp vanilla essence
2 tbsp brown sugar
½ tsp ground cloves
1 tsp cinnamon

Preheat the oven to 200°C. To make the cinnamon crème fraîche, whisk together the crème fraîche and one teaspoon of cinnamon until light and fluffy. Refrigerate until chilled.

For the plum and almond tart, combine the flour, baking powder, almonds, butter, egg yolk and salt in the bowl of a food processor or in a large bowl and using a hand-mixer or mixing by hand, blend until crumbled to make almond flour. Toss together the plums, lime zest, vanilla essence, brown sugar, cloves and cinnamon in a second bowl.

Press two-thirds of the almond flour into the bottom of a greased 25 cm springform pan and arrange the plums on top in an even layer, beginning along the exterior and working inwards. Sprinkle with the remaining almond flour and bake until the plum juices are bubbling and the topping is golden brown, for about 45 minutes. Cool to room temperature, transfer to a plate, cut into slices and serve with a dollop of cinnamon crème fraîche.

Eithna's By the Sea

In 1990, Eithna O'Sullivan opened her restaurant Eithna's By the Sea just down the road from Strandhill, where Shells Café is located, on a street overlooking the harbour in Mullaghmore, County Sligo, She has been vigilantly sourcing products from local food producers and tirelessly championing Irish food traditions ever since.

Her pioneering efforts to conjure an abiding love for the ocean's riches in Irish customers and tourists alike by transforming them into recipes like seaweed pesto and carrageen moss chocolate cake has transformed her restaurant with its exposed limestone walls, arched windows and façade painted with ocean waves breaking in every shade of blue into a destination for food lovers from around the world.

With a lithe voice and gentle disposition that belies her fierce devotion to the region's fishermen and foragers, Eithna, who earned a culinary arts degree by writing a thesis about why seaweed should be considered an artisan food product, says, 'I like knowing that my restaurant is a place where those who forage along the seashore and fish our waters can bring their products. Their hard work is appreciated and it's rewarding to work together to keep our Irish traditions alive.'

Drannie Rhatigan
Seaweed Walk
talk and Lunch
Starts 11am at
Eithna's

Welcome to Eithna's
By the Sea

Seafood Tasting
Plate (Mussels, Mackerel,
Prawns, Crab Claws & Smoked Salmon)
.... €13.95

Mackerel & chips
.... €12.50

Trio of Dessert:
Carrageen Moss pudding,
Nori blancmange & Chocolate
Brownie   €6.95

Chicken Ciabatta €8.50

'I LIKE KNOWING THAT
MY RESTAURANT IS A
PLACE WHERE THOSE
WHO FORAGE ALONG
THE SEASHORE AND
FISH OUR WATERS CAN
BRING THEIR PRODUCTS.
THEIR HARD WORK IS
APPRECIATED AND
IT'S REWARDING TO
WORK TOGETHER
TO KEEP OUR IRISH
TRADITIONS ALIVE.'

" I longed for a sod of earth from some field I knew, something of Sligo to hold in my hand. "

WILLIAM BUTLER YEATS

Sligo
TRAVEL GUIDE

William Butler Yeats was born in Dublin but much of his childhood was spent in County Sligo, a location that features prominently in his poetry. There are tributes to Yeats throughout the county and devotees flock here to indulge in the favourite haunts of the beloved scribe. Between stops along the Yeats trail, visit the town of Sligo itself, an industrious town with a storied past. Browse the lovely antique and craft shops along Grattan and Castle Streets, such as Cosgroves Deli and The Curiosity Shop, check out the Sligo Flea Market for quirky finds and local crafts and pop into pubs like McGlynns, Foley's or Shoot the Crows to catch one of the trad sessions that has made Sligo renowned the world over.

Strandhill is ideal for a beach stroll, a sandwich at Shells Café and a dip in a warm seaweed bath at VOYA. Woodville Farm, just outside Strandhill, offers tours of its traditional small family farm, and Coney Island, which is connected to the mainland by a strip of shore when the tide is out, entices with its beaches and all the peace and quiet this little corner of the Wild Atlantic Way can muster. Hike up Knocknarea to visit Medb's Cairn and take in the beauty of the five counties that can be viewed from this spectacular vantage point. Eithna's By Sea in the holiday village of Mullaghmore in the shadow of Benbulben Mountain is also worth a visit; make sure to stop off at Mullaghmore Head for a heart-palpitating view over the sea. At Lough Gill, where Yeats said 'peace comes dropping slow', there's another breathtaking view from Dooney Rock. A wander through Slish Wood and a stop at Tobernalt Holy Well are also interesting sights to take in during a stay in County Sligo.

'THE ISLAND PROVIDED
FOR US JUST AS IT HAS
DONE FOR GENERATIONS;
WE JUST HAD TO LISTEN
CLOSELY TO WHAT IT WAS
TRYING TO TELL US.'

3 | Achill Island Sea Salt

Kieran and Marjorie O'Malley

Kieran O'Malley, a secondary school principal and proud member of the Achill Pipe Band, which he co-founded in 2007, and his wife Marjorie feared their children would have to move away from their home on Achill Island in search of work if they did not sort something out that ensured a secure future for them. Emigration has long been the plight of the younger generation of islanders, who find little promise of steady work on an island that has suffered from business closures and a lack of resources. But it turned out that for the O'Malleys and their children, the solution was all around them.

'Marjorie and I had an epiphany one day when we looked out at the pristine ocean that surrounded us and collectively knew what we were going to do.' Marjorie had caught a documentary profiling sea salt production in the United Kingdom at the same time that Kieran was reading a history book on the early nineteenth-century salt factory of Polranny, which had long since closed its doors on a tradition that was once commonplace on their island. Inspired, the O'Malleys, together with their eldest son, Sean, started their company, Achill Island Sea Salt, in 2013.

Word quickly spread throughout Ireland that there was a company hand-harvesting ocean water from the bays of Keel and Dooagh to produce a flaky, snow-white sea salt that virtually melted on the tongue or over the food it was sprinkled upon. Their company has gone from strength to strength in the short time since its inception. The production centre has moved from the family's kitchen over their stove in pots, which, Kieran explains, were easily corroded by the salt, to a facility next door where they were able to install stainless steel mechanically controlled evaporators and dehydrators.

There are no chemicals or caking agents added to the unrefined Achill Island Sea Salt and since it's harvested from one of the most unspoilt coastlines in the world, the end result is as pristine as the waters from which it is sourced. Their salt has garnered several awards and maintains a prominent place in the larders of home and restaurant kitchens and shop shelves throughout the nation. 'It has been gratifying to know that our hard work to create a product that is Achill Island through and through has been so well received by the Irish people. We wanted to produce something that our children would be proud of and establish a tradition that they could carry on should they choose to do so,' Kieran says as he looks out over the ocean lapping at this bare feet, a bucket of ocean water sitting beside them. 'I think we have done that. The island provided for us just as it has done for generations; we just had to listen closely to what it was trying to tell us.'

ROASTED PARSNIP SOUP WITH GREEN APPLES AND HAZELNUTS

Parsnips are often overlooked for the tangerine-hued enticements of the carrot, but these humble root vegetables with their elegant white complexion are just as appealing as their more ornate cousins. Apples add a little lustre and hazelnuts a bit of earthiness and texture to this silky soup that celebrates the parsnip in all its winter white glory. If you would like a lighter soup, swap out the double cream for more stock and omit the butter altogether. As a final flourish, sprinkle a few flakes of sea salt over the surface of the soup for a crunchy saline finish.

SERVES 4
PREPARATION TIME: 45 MINUTES

3 tbsp olive oil
1 tbsp cumin seeds
1 tbsp ground coriander
1 tsp chilli flakes
700 g parsnips, peeled and roughly chopped
2 medium onions, roughly chopped
2 cloves garlic
500 ml double cream
500 ml chicken or vegetable stock
30 g butter
1 tbsp freshly squeezed lemon juice, plus additional for seasoning
salt and freshly ground black pepper, to taste

To serve:
leaves from 1 sprig thyme
green apple, roughly chopped
hazelnuts, roughly chopped and toasted
sea salt
crusty bread

Preheat the oven to 200°C. In a large bowl, stir together the oil, cumin, coriander and chilli flakes. Add the parsnips, onions and garlic and stir until everything is glistening and coated well. Arrange in an even layer on a tin foil-lined baking tray and roast until the parsnips are caramelised, for about 30 minutes.

Transfer to a food processor and add the double cream, stock, butter and lemon juice. Purée until smooth and season with salt and pepper along with additional lemon juice, if desired.

To serve, heat up in a pot. Ladle into a bowl and garnish with thyme, green apples and hazelnuts and sprinkle with sea salt. Serve with generous hunks of crusty bread.

BRAISED JUNIPER AND BLACK PEPPER VENISON WITH COLCANNON

Hunting in Ireland goes hand in hand with the autumn and winter months when the forests of the west teem with deer. The red, fallow and silka are all common but the red is the only native Irish species remaining. This recipe celebrates the hearty flavour of venison with a slow braise that gives the flavour time to find its footing, and what better way to discover it than in a rich broth of peppery red wine? Take your time with this recipe and your guests will thank you for it as the aromas of juniper and anise fill the air. Redcurrant jam energises the peppery notes, or try rowan jam, which, with its jewelled tangerine glow, is a welcome way to invite Ireland to the table. There is no better side for this dish than colcannon, a recipe that celebrates the virtues of the cabbage and the potato, two vegetables that it would be impossible to imagine Ireland without.

SERVES 4
PREPARATION TIME: 1 HOUR 45 MINUTES

For the juniper and black pepper venison:
30 g butter
1 large onion, roughly chopped
2 celery stalks, roughly chopped
1 large carrot, peeled and roughly chopped
2 cloves garlic, thinly sliced
1 kg venison shoulder or loin, cut into 2 cm cubes
pinch of salt
45 g plain flour
1 tbsp freshly ground black pepper
400 ml dry red wine (Pinot Noir or Syrah work well)
5 sage leaves, finely chopped
2 bay leaves
1 star anise pod
6 juniper berries
3 tbsp redcurrant or rowan jam
500 ml beef stock
salt and freshly ground black pepper, to taste

For the colcannon:
4 large Rooster or white potatoes
1 small head green cabbage, cored, quartered and sliced into 1 cm strips
30 g butter
3 tbsp milk, plus additional as necessary
2 spring onions, thinly sliced
salt and freshly ground black pepper, to taste

Preheat the oven to 180°C. In a heavy-bottom casserole over a medium-high heat, melt one tablespoon of butter and sauté the onion, celery and carrots until the onions are translucent and the carrots are tender. Add the garlic and sauté for one more minute, then remove from the heat and set aside. Season the venison with salt. Combine the flour, black pepper and venison in a plastic bag, seal it and give it a good long shake to evenly coat the venison cubes.

Melt the remaining tablespoon of the butter in a sauté pan over a high heat and once the butter is bubbling, sauté the venison until golden brown on all sides. Do not overcrowd the pan, as this will prevent even browning, so work in batches if necessary. Add the browned meat to the casserole. Deglaze the bottom of the pan with a splash of the red wine to scrape up any brown bits that may have formed. Add the sage, bay leaves, star anise, juniper, jam, stock and remaining wine and bring to a lazy simmer. Pour the hot cooking liquid into the casserole and stir to combine. Transfer to the oven and braise until the venison is fall-apart tender, for about 90 minutes.

While the venison cooks, prepare the colcannon by bringing a saucepan of salted water and the potatoes to a boil. Reduce the heat to low and simmer until the potatoes are fork tender, for about 15 minutes. Bring another saucepan of salted water and the cabbage to a boil. Reduce the heat and simmer until the cabbage is tender, for about 10 minutes. Drain the cabbage, add one tablespoon of butter and stir until the cabbage glistens. Drain the potatoes and slip off the skins while they are still hot. In a saucepan, combine the remaining butter, milk and spring onions and bring to a gentle simmer. Add to the potatoes and beat until fluffy and smooth. Stir in the cabbage and season with salt and pepper.

Remove the venison from the oven and season with salt and pepper. Serve a spoonful alongside the colcannon on a cold winter's night beside a raging peat fire.

BARBECUE PULLED PORK AND PICKLED RADISH BAP

This recipe requires a little time but there's nothing like a pulled pork sandwich for lunch after the enticing porcine aroma has filled the house all morning. This is a weekend dish that invites a low and slow approach but it's well worth it in the end. The quick pickled radishes offer a bit of moxie and the spring onion champ pulls it all together. Champ is a frequent headliner on the Irish table. It's closely related to colcannon, that king of Irish cabbage dishes, but cabbage is swapped out for spring onions in champ.

MAKES ABOUT 8 SANDWICHES
PREPARATION TIME: 9 HOURS

For the barbecue pulled pork:
2 kg pork shoulder, boned, with rind still
  attached, and bound with twine (ask
  your butcher to prepare this for you if
  necessary)
salt, as needed
2 tbsp ground cumin
2 tbsp yellow mustard powder
2 tbsp smoked paprika
1 tbsp garlic powder
1 tbsp freshly ground black pepper
2 tbsp brown sugar
6 bay leaves
2 medium onions, thinly sliced
1 litre water
4 tbsp red wine vinegar
3 tbsp ketchup
1 tbsp honey
1 tbsp Worcestershire sauce

For the pickled radishes:
12 radishes, thinly sliced
4 tbsp water
8 tbsp apple cider vinegar
2 tbsp caster sugar

For the spring onion champ:
4 large Rooster or white potatoes,
  roughly chopped
30 g butter
6 spring onions, roughly chopped
4 tbsp double cream
salt and freshly ground black pepper,
  to taste

To serve:
8 baps
lettuce leaves
red onion, thinly sliced
sea salt

Preheat the oven to 160°C. Season the pork shoulder with salt. Combine the ground cumin, mustard powder, smoked paprika, garlic powder, black pepper and one tablespoon of brown sugar in a small bowl and stir until incorporated. Rub all over the pork shoulder, ensuring that no nook or cranny is neglected. Scatter the bay leaves and onions on the bottom of a large roasting tin and place the pork, fat side up, in the centre of the tin. Pour one litre of water into the tin and cover securely with tin foil.

Roast slowly until cooked through, for about seven hours. Be careful when lifting off the tin foil to prevent a steam burn. Using tongs, remove the fat and discard (or reserve for another use). Once the pork is cool enough to handle, shred it by hand into small pieces. Discard the bay leaves, then transfer the cooking juices and onions to a blender and purée until smooth. In a large bowl, combine the cooking juices, red wine vinegar, ketchup, remaining brown sugar, honey and Worcestershire sauce and stir to combine. Add the pulled pork and stir until it is well coated with the barbecue sauce. Next, transfer it to a saucepan, cover and cook over a low heat until the meat takes on the flavour of the barbecue sauce through and through, stirring every 10 minutes or so for about one hour.

While the pork cooks, place the radishes in a heatproof bowl. In a saucepan, combine the water and the apple cider vinegar and bring to a boil. Remove from the heat, add the caster sugar and stir until dissolved. Pour over the radishes and let cool to room temperature. Drain once ready to use or store in a covered container in the refrigerator for up to two weeks.

As the radishes pickle, make the spring onion champ by bringing a saucepan of salted water and the potatoes to a boil. Reduce the heat to a gentle simmer and cook until the potatoes are fork tender, for about 15 minutes. While the potatoes cook, melt one tablespoon of the butter in a sauté pan over a medium-high heat and sauté the spring onions until tender, for about four minutes. Drain the potatoes once they are ready, return them to the saucepan along with the spring onions, double cream and remaining butter and combine with a potato masher until creamy. Season with salt and pepper and keep warm.

Slice open a bap or a roll of your choice, top with a lettuce leaf, a few red onion slices and a generous spoonful of pulled pork. Garnish with slices of pickled radish and serve with a bowl of spring onion champ sprinkled with sea salt.

LAZY SUNDAY SAUSAGE AND SPINACH ROLLS WITH HONEY MUSTARD SAUCE

Sausage rolls are a beloved snack or quick on-the-go lunch in Ireland, and why not? They're filling, comforting and fun to eat, especially when slathered in mustard or, as in this recipe, honey mustard. Feel free to make your own sausage but on a busy day, pre-made sausage is the way to go. Be sure to pop it out of its casing in order to perfectly accommodate the length of your puff pastry. Then there's nothing to it but a little rolling, egg-washing and baking. This is a fun weekend snack on a rainy day or an easy lunch on a rushed afternoon.

MAKES 2 LARGE ROLLS
PREPARATION TIME: 1 HOUR

For the filling:
4 large sausages
1 small handful breadcrumbs
15 g butter
200 g spinach

For the pastry:
1 egg, beaten
splash of milk
2 sheets ready-made puff pastry
sea salt

For the honey mustard sauce:
4 tbsp Dijon mustard
1 tbsp honey

To make the sausage and spinach filing, use a sharp paring knife to slit the sausage casings and remove the meat from inside. Mix it together with the breadcrumbs in a bowl using your hands. Melt the butter in a sauté pan and sauté the spinach until just wilted.

Preheat the oven to 200°C. To prepare the pastry, beat the egg and the milk in a small bowl and set aside. Lay the puff pastry onto a floured work surface and beat it gently with a rolling pin. This will prevent the pastry from puffing too much while baking. Cut the pastry lengthwise into two rectangles and brush each end with the beaten egg. Arrange half the spinach over one rectangle and then the other one. Shape the meat into two sausage shapes as long as the width of the rectangle and about 3 cm wide and place on top of the spinach. Roll the pastry around the sausage to form a roll and pinch together the sides, scoring it along the seam after it is secured. Refrigerate for 20 minutes to stiffen the pastry and encourage it to stay together while cooking. Brush the top of each roll with a little beaten egg and score the top to enable the release of air while it cooks. Sprinkle with sea salt, then bake until the rolls are golden brown and the pastry is cooked all the way through, for about 30 minutes.

As the rolls cook, whisk together the mustard and honey in a small bowl until slightly runny, adding a bit of water if necessary to achieve the desired consistency. Remove the rolls from the oven, slice into quarters and serve with the honey mustard sauce. They're sure to bring comfort to even the chilliest afternoon.

CHOCOLATE AND WHISKEY FLOURLESS CAKE WITH BLACKBERRY SAUCE AND SEA SALT

Blackberry bushes flourish in the dense hedgerows of western Ireland and there is nothing better than plucking a few and popping them into your mouth while on a hike beneath the Irish summer sun. The tanginess of the blackberry sauce pairs well with the chocolate cake that is extra-rich in the absence of flour. The sauce will keep in the refrigerator for at least a week and freezes well indefinitely. It's wonderful drizzled over pancakes or on scones slathered in butter. The sea salt provides a crunchy finish to this decadent dessert.

MAKES 1 x 20 CM CAKE
PREPARATION TIME: 45 MINUTES

For the chocolate and whiskey flourless cake:
125 g dark chocolate, roughly chopped
125 g butter, plus additional for greasing
1 tbsp Irish whiskey
100 g caster sugar
3 large eggs, beaten
3 tbsp hazelnuts, finely chopped and toasted
1 tbsp cocoa powder

For the blackberry sauce:
450 g blackberries
65 g caster sugar
1 tbsp freshly squeezed lemon juice
5 g cornflour

To serve:
1 tbsp cocoa powder
sea salt

Preheat the oven to 190°C. Cut a round of parchment the same size as the bottom of a 20 cm baking pan, butter the parchment and place in the bottom of the pan. Bring a saucepan of water to a lazy simmer, place a bowl on top of the pan and add the chocolate and butter and whisk constantly to melt the chocolate. Once shiny and emulsified, remove from the heat, add the whiskey and sugar and whisk until combined. Next, add the eggs and whisk until incorporated. Stir in the hazelnuts and the cocoa powder and pour the batter into the prepared pan. Bake on the centre rack of the oven until the top layer of cake has formed a thin crust, for about 25 minutes.

While the cake bakes, prepare the blackberry sauce by combining the blackberries and sugar in a saucepan and bringing to a gentle simmer over a medium heat while stirring frequently to break down the berries and prevent scorching. Simmer until the sugar is dissolved, for about three minutes. Mix the lemon juice and cornflour and whisk into the blackberry sauce. Strain through a sieve, if desired, and cool to room temperature before serving. The sauce keeps in a covered container in the refrigerator for up to one week or frozen indefinitely.

Remove the cake from the oven and let cool for 10 minutes before inverting onto a plate. Dust the cake with cocoa powder. Cut the cake into slices, drizzle with blackberry sauce and sprinkle with sea salt.

Irish Honey

Beekeeping is one of the oldest food traditions in the world and Ireland was no exception. Bees and their residual honey have always played an integral part in Irish agricultural production and cooking traditions. Most rural households in ancient Ireland kept bees and their honey was used as the primary sweetener until cane sugar was introduced to the island in the sixteenth century. There were laws established, known as the Bechbretha or 'Bee Judgements', to denote everything from the rules surrounding hive ownership to the amount that a hive owner had to pay if his bees stung someone. Bee hives were even offered as tribute to the Gaelic kings. Irish monks were renowned beekeepers and beeswax candles alighted homes, churches and businesses throughout the nation. Beeswax was even used as a tablet for young scholars to practise their penmanship upon.

The early Irish were so enamoured with honey that there are accounts that tell of dinner parties where small bowls filled with honey were arranged next to each plate on the table into which each and every bite of food consumed was dipped before it reached the mouth. Honey was mixed together with lard as a condiment or stirred into milk and tea before drinking. It was a popular marinade and also found its way into baked goods like breads and scones. It was also fermented to produce mead, one of the island's most popular libations for centuries.

There might not be a hive on the property of every household in rural Ireland like there once was, but beekeeping is still fundamentally important to the sustenance of food and agriculture in Ireland. Irish honey producers thrive throughout the nation, not least along the Wild Atlantic Way, where bees revel in the wild berries and flowers that flourish in the hedgerows, forests and home gardens.

"When I come out on the road of a morning, when I have had a night's sleep and perhaps a breakfast, and the sun lights a hill on the distance, a hill I know I shall walk across an hour or two thence, and it is green and silken to my eye, and the clouds have begun their slow, fat rolling journey across the sky, no land in the world can inspire such love in a common man."

FRANK DELANEY

Mayo
TRAVEL GUIDE

Achill Island is connected to Mayo by a bridge a few miles from the charming gateway village of Newport where you'll find Kelly's Butchers, a famed artisan butchers run by the Kelly family since 1930, now run by brothers Seán and Seamus and their children. Their award-winning Irish black pudding is worth the journey alone. Stop by the Blue Bicycle Tea Rooms before leaving town for a pot of tea, a slice of homemade cake or a cup of carrageen and vegetable soup.

From Newport, you can visit Westport, where visitors stop to enjoy some of Ireland's best seafood chowder at the West Bar and Restaurant or grab a pint at world-renowned Matt Molloy's. Trad sessions take place here virtually every night and the pub's owner, Matt Malloy of the Chieftains, sometimes joins in on his flute to inspire a bit of craic. Stop by Cabots of Westport to pick up a few goodies from Redmond Cabot, such as his beetroot and sage dip or Achill Island smoked mackerel pâté. About 15 minutes from Westport is Café Rua in Castlebar, one of County Mayo's most ardent promoters of locally sourced food products.

Down the road from Castlebar is Cong, location of John Wayne's iconic movie *The Quiet Man*. Featured in the film, Pat Cohan's Bar now boasts a lovely menu comprised of local produce, lamb, beef, cheese and beer. Cong is adjacent to magnificent Ashford Castle and the best way to get there is through a walk along the river in Cong Woods. Ashford's restaurants, including the cosy Lodge at Ashford Castle, pride themselves on using primarily local ingredients. There's also a falconry school on the property that is an unforgettable experience not to be missed.

While exploring the area, look for Fionntan Gogarty's Wildwood Vinegars, comprised of such sublime flavours as fuchsia, elderflower, mountain heather and wild rose petal. If you're in need of a way to burn through a few calories after indulging in Mayo's wealth of gastronomic pleasures, grab your walking stick and follow the pilgrims to the top of Croagh Patrick, which affords extraordinary views of the entire region. If you decide to venture on to Achill, one of the best ways to get there is via bicycle along the Great Western Greenway, a 26-mile bike path that stretches from Westport to Achill Island.

MARTIN CALVEY
IDENTIFIED THE
QUALITIES OF
ADAPTABILITY,
RESILIENCY AND
EXCEPTIONAL FLAVOUR
IN THE ISLAND'S SHEEP
DECADES BEFORE THE
CONCEPT OF BRANDING
EXISTED.

4 | Achill Mountain Lamb

Martin Calvey and Family

The Blackface Mountain lamb of Achill Island roam freely over 20,000 acres of 'commanage', land that is shared by the residents of this island and connected by a bridge to mainland Ireland. They graze on grasses rich in samphire, seaweed and calcium along the island's shore before venturing into the mountains for heather and other wild herbs, resulting in meat that is 'ocean salty and heather sweet', according to Martina Calvey. She's one of Martin Calvey's eight daughters and two sons who sell Achill Mountain Lamb from the island's last remaining abattoir.

The family's thriving business, which also includes a pantry called Top Drawer and Pantry run by Martina's sister, Maeve, that sells products like Achill sea salted oil, wild mint butter and Achill lamb sausage rolls, was founded over 60 years ago by father Martin. The visionary, who herds his black-faced sheep with the help of his rambunctious border collie Rosie and grandson Peter, identified the qualities of adaptability, resiliency and exceptional flavour in the island's sheep decades before the concept of branding existed.

Martin was only a boy when he realised that the sheep he had grown up watching graze the rolling hills and mineral-rich grasses along the beaches of Achill were something special. Today, the Calveys' hand-butchered sheep are prised on restaurant menus and in home kitchens throughout Ireland. Martin says, 'I'm very proud of our sheep and the meat that we sell because it embodies the unique qualities of Achill Island. It's a tradition that I hope will continue long after I'm gone. I hope that it's a legacy that endures.'

His daughter Martina says that the sheep of Achill have withstood the plundering of industrialisation that wiped out other customs on the island, such as fishing in wooden currach boats. 'People don't always want something that reminds them of the past. They want to move forward and make progress.' She pauses to survey the waves crashing into the island's ashen cliffs before continuing, 'But I have hope that the tradition of Achill Mountain Lamb will continue because it not only represents the past, but is a symbol of the future too.'

LAMB BURGERS WITH CREAMY RED CABBAGE SLAW

No one does lamb burgers better than Ireland and the best way to prepare these is to have your butcher freshly mince your lamb meat before taking it home. Small family-owned butchers might be a rare fixture in the landscapes of rural communities in other parts of the world, but in Ireland they continue to thrive, supported by a population that values and invests in family-owned businesses. In this recipe, lamb is paired with a whimsical purple cabbage slaw that provides a welcome snap. The burger is slathered in rosemary aioli, a Provençal condiment with endless variations, its foundation being lemon, garlic, egg yolks and olive oil. Make an extra-large batch and serve it drizzled over smoked salmon on bagels the next day or in a sandwich or even with roasted potatoes.

SERVES 4
PREPARATION TIME: 30 MINUTES

For the lamb burgers:
1 kg lamb mince
2 tsp garlic powder
2 tsp onion powder
1 tbsp cumin seeds
salt and freshly ground black pepper,
  to taste
2 tbsp vegetable oil

For the creamy red cabbage slaw:
4 tbsp mayonnaise
1 tbsp apple cider vinegar
1 tsp mustard seeds
1 tbsp olive oil
1 small red onion, halved and thinly
  sliced
1 small head red cabbage, cored,
  quartered and thinly sliced
1 green apple, cored and roughly
  chopped

For the rosemary aioli:
1 tbsp rosemary, finely chopped
1 clove garlic, finely chopped
pinch of salt
1 egg yolk
2 tsp Dijon mustard
400 ml olive oil
freshly squeezed lemon juice, to taste

To serve:
4 burger buns or baps
1 medium onion, sliced
cucumber pickles
sea salt

In a bowl, combine the lamb, garlic and onion powders and cumin and mix with your hands until just incorporated. Don't overmix or it will become stiff and lose some of its juiciness when fried. Season with salt and pepper and form into four patties. Heat the vegetable oil over a medium-high heat in a sauté pan and fry the burgers until cooked to your liking, flipping once to encourage browning on both sides.

To make the slaw, whisk together the mayonnaise, vinegar, mustard seeds and olive oil. Toss together the red onions, cabbage and apples, then add the mayonnaise and stir until everything is well coated.

For the aioli, use a mortar and pestle or the back of a spoon to smash together the rosemary, garlic and enough salt to form a paste. Stir together the egg yolk and mustard in a medium-sized bowl, then add the garlic paste and stir to incorporate.

Add about one-third of the olive oil in a slow, steady stream and whisk vigorously to emulsify the aioli. Once it reaches this stage, add the rest of your oil in the same slow, steady stream, pausing frequently to ensure that the aioli is thickening up properly. Once all of the oil has been incorporated, whisk in the lemon juice and season with additional salt, if desired.

Slice open the buns and toast them in a warm oven. Line the bottom of each bun with onions and cucumber pickles and spoon a generous amount of aioli over them. Top with a burger and a spoonful of the slaw, or serve the slaw on the side for a less messy meal. Either way, be sure to sprinkle everything with sea salt for a crunchy finish.

SUMMER BERRY DUTCH BABY

There's a restaurant on Achill Island called the Beehive Café that hums with activity from the wee hours of the morning. It's the ideal place to jumpstart a day tour of Achill with a cup of robust coffee or pot of Irish tea accompanied by one of the restaurant's many homemade breakfast goodies. This recipe is a tribute to the Beehive Café's magical ability to start the morning right.

The name 'Dutch baby' derives from the German immigrant group in America referred to as 'Pennsylvania Dutch', a corruption of the German moniker 'Deutsch', so this dish really has nothing to do with the Netherlands, despite its name. But while the Dutch baby might have German origins, there is no better catchall for the summer berries that flourish in western Ireland than this light and airy giant popover. This delicious breakfast treat is an ideal way to celebrate the nation's bounty of summertime berries on an inviting canvas. The key is to serve it quickly before the edges fall, but even after they do, there is nothing more fun (or easier) than this breakfast dish on a weekend morning. Bananas are also a nice way to dress up this recipe, as are apples, blueberries, raspberries, plums or, if the day calls for going all out, chocolate with a dusting of icing sugar.

MAKES 1 DUTCH BABY
PREPARATION TIME: 40 MINUTES

45 g butter, softened, plus additional for
  serving
115 g plain flour
120 ml milk
2 large eggs, beaten
3 tbsp caster sugar
1 tsp vanilla essence
½ tsp cinnamon, plus additional for
  serving
zest of ½ lemon
pinch of salt
handful blackberries
4 or 5 strawberries, cut into wedges

To serve:
lemon wedges

Preheat the oven to 200°C. In a cast-iron skillet or heavy-bottom frying pan, add two tablespoons of the butter and place the pan in the oven for 10 minutes. While the pan heats up, combine the flour, milk, eggs, remaining butter, sugar, vanilla essence, cinnamon, lemon zest and salt and whisk vigorously until combined and slightly frothy, for about 30 seconds.

Remove the pan from the oven and pour the batter into it.

Arrange the berries on top of the batter (they will become slightly immersed) and return the pan to the oven. Bake until the sides are puffy, risen and golden brown, for about 30 minutes. Serve quickly for full dramatic effect with additional knobs of butter, lemon wedges and a sprinkle of cinnamon.

SWEET POTATO, WHITE BEAN AND LAMB STEW

Martin Calvey of Achill Mountain Lamb knows a thing or two (or ten) about lamb and we're sure he would approve of this easy stew that provides the perfect vehicle for chunks of succulent lamb shoulder. Of course, stewing beef makes a fine substitute but nothing quite compares to lamb, especially when paired with sweet potato, a generous splash of dry white wine and a cap of toasted breadcrumbs to soak up all those juices. Lentils or chickpeas make good substitutes for the cannellini beans and don't forget the crusty bread for dipping.

SERVES 4
PREPARATION TIME: 55 MINUTES

1 kg boneless lamb shoulder, cut into bite-size pieces
10 g plain flour
salt and freshly ground black pepper, to taste
1 tbsp vegetable oil
1 small onion, roughly chopped
2 cloves garlic, thinly sliced
120 ml dry white wine (Pinot Grigio or Sauvignon Blanc work well)
500 ml chicken or vegetable stock
1 cinnamon stick
1 large sweet potato, peeled and roughly chopped
1 x 400 g tin cannellini beans, drained and rinsed

To serve:
breadcrumbs, toasted
crusty bread with creamy butter

In a plastic bag, toss together the lamb and flour until the meat is well coated. Season with salt and pepper. In a heavy-bottom saucepan, heat the oil over a medium-high heat and sauté the onions and garlic until the garlic is aromatic. Add the lamb and sear until it is golden brown on all sides, for about three minutes. Add the wine and bring to a boil, scraping up any brown bits that have formed on the bottom of the pot.

Next, add the stock, cinnamon and sweet potato and bring to a boil. Reduce the heat, cover and let the stew bubble away. Add the beans after 20 minutes, then allow the meat and sweet potato to simmer until they are tender, for about a further 25 minutes. Season with salt and pepper. Ladle into bowls, sprinkle with toasted breadcrumbs and serve with crusty bread slathered with creamy butter on the side.

SLOE GIN FIZZ

Sloe berries, from the blackthorn tree, thrive in the hedgerows of western Ireland each summer but these taut, amethyst-coloured berries are not ready for harvest until after the first frost, which entices their sweet juices to emerge. To make sloe gin, prick the berries with a needle to encourage their juices to flow or freeze them overnight and bash them with a rolling pin before immersing in gin and sugar. Either way, the next part of the sloe gin recipe is the most challenging: waiting. To properly infuse your gin, give the sloes at least three months to work their magic, vigorously shaking the tightly sealed container about once a week to encourage the infusion. If they are harvested and infused at the right time, the gin, with its heliotrope hue, will be ready just in time for the holidays, when there is no better time to indulge in this regal spirit. Of course, sloe gin is also available ready-made at many off-licenses, but if you're fortunate enough to discover sloes in your hedgerows, make your own. It will make your enjoyment of this sloe gin fizz with its bubbly cap and amethyst colour all the more virtuous.

This recipe calls for simple syrup, a combination of equal parts water and caster sugar brought to a boil and simmered until the sugar is dissolved. Cool to room temperature before using.

MAKES 1 COCKTAIL
PREPARATION TIME: 5 MINUTES (PLUS THREE MONTHS TO MAKE THE SLOE GIN)

60 ml sloe gin
1 tbsp freshly squeezed lemon juice
1 tbsp simple syrup
club soda, as needed

Combine the gin, lemon juice and simple syrup in a cocktail shaker filled to the top with ice and give it a robust shake. Strain into a chilled tall glass and pour the club soda on top. Be a little wild with your pour to encourage the fizz.

ROAST BEEF AND VEGETABLES WITH PORT GRAVY AND HORSERADISH CREAM

The Calveys' business might be focused on lamb, but the whole family would agree that sometimes there's nothing better on a Sunday afternoon than gathering the family around the table for a beef roast. England may boast about its Sunday roast, but the Irish execute it with just as much gusto and passion as their neighbours. There is no better place to enjoy a Sunday roast than in a cosy thatched pub along the sea in western Ireland, but no matter where you find yourself in the world, this recipe is a lovely way to celebrate the close of a week surrounded by the ones you love.

SERVES 4
PREPARATION TIME: 1 ½ HOURS

For the roast beef and vegetables:
1 ½ kg high-quality centre-cut beef tenderloin
1 large onion, roughly chopped
2 carrots, roughly chopped (leave the peel on for rustic effect and more flavour)
2 celery stalks, roughly chopped
10 baby potatoes, skin on
cloves from 1 garlic bulb, peeled
1 bay leaf
2 sprigs thyme
olive oil, as needed
salt and freshly ground black pepper, to taste

For the port gravy:
½ bottle high-quality port
45 g butter, chilled
salt and freshly ground black pepper, to taste

For the horseradish crème fraîche:
240 ml crème fraîche
2 tbsp horseradish sauce
salt and freshly ground black pepper, to taste

Remove the beef from the refrigerator around 45 minutes before it's needed to bring it to room temperature before roasting. Preheat the oven to 240°C. In a roasting tin, combine the onions, carrots, celery, potatoes, garlic, bay leaf and thyme, drizzle with olive oil and season with salt and pepper. Rub the beef in all its crevasses with oil, salt and pepper and place atop the veggies. After 15 minutes in the oven, reduce the heat to 200°C and roast for an hour for a medium roast. Shave off 10 minutes if you prefer it a little rarer or add 15 minutes if you're a well-done kind of gathering.

Using tongs, carefully remove the roast beef from the pan and place on a rack, covering it with a clean tea towel while it rests for about 15 more minutes. Turn over once during the resting period to evenly distribute its cooking juices. Remove the veggies from the pan and keep them warm in a bowl.

Discard the bay leaf and thyme and place the roasting tin with its cooking juices over a medium heat on the hob. Add the port and bring to a simmer, scraping up the brown bits on the bottom of the tin for an extra-flavourful sauce. Reduce the gravy until it's thick enough to coat the back of a wooden spoon, then add a knob of chilled butter and stir until completely incorporated before adding one more and doing the same thing, and then another. Season the gravy with salt and pepper.

While the gravy reduces, make the horseradish cream by whisking the crème fraîche in a large bowl until it starts to thicken and gentle peaks form. Add the prepared horseradish, salt and pepper and whisk to incorporate. Serve the roast beef surrounded by the roasted vegetables on a beautiful serving platter with the port gravy and horseradish cream in lovely little bowls on the side. Be sure to accompany it with plenty of red wine, good cheer and a warm fireplace to keep the festive vibe going long into the night.

Foraging

There is no better way to explore the hedgerows and coastal areas of Ireland, such as Achill Island, than with a basket in hand ready to receive the berries, nuts and flowers that flourish there throughout the seasons. There are sloes for gin, rosehips for syrup, fuchsia for vinegar, elderberries for wine, spirits and jams, and elderflowers for cordial. There are wild garlic, nettles, chickweed, hazelnuts, watercress and blackberries. In the forests there are mushrooms waiting to be discovered and strewn along the seashore await dozens of varieties of seaweed.

There is something to be discovered during every season of the year in Ireland because it rarely becomes cold enough to quell growth and it's a delight to anticipate what edible hedgerow, forest or ocean feast awaits just around the seasonal bend. Syrups, spirits, jams and cordials made from foraged foods make such wonderful gifts because they not only taste sublime, but they embody the spirit of Ireland too.

"Dance first. Think later. It's the natural order. "

SAMUEL BECKETT

Achill Island
TRAVEL GUIDE

Achill Island is Ireland's largest island and is connected to the mainland via the Michael Davitt Bridge, originally constructed in the 1880s. It is here that sheep roam free along the expansive beaches where kite-surfers, kayakers and surfers revel in the waves of this aquatic wonderland. Take a boat ride to the Seal Caves near Dugort, so named because of the seal population that once flourished here before sport hunters decimated the population. The occasional seal can still be spotted bobbing near the caves, but the cavernous space inside is enough to justify the visit. Golf fanatics can indulge in the nine-hole Achill Island Golf Course near Keel Strand with the ocean mist on their faces as they dodge the sheep who wander along the beach to munch on the samphire beds.

Climb the glistening cone of Slievemore Mountain, comprised of quartz and mica, for the island's most stunning (and staggering) views. In Slievemore's shadow, the Deserted Village with its abandoned stone houses reminds visitors of a time not so long ago when farmers shifted their homes with the seasons in order to enable their cattle to graze in the most fertile fields. Nearby are 5,000-year-old Megalithic tombs that beguile with their echo of a pre-Christian past, embodying the mystical side of Ireland that still entices visitors millennia later.

Biking and horseback riding are great ways to get the most out of a visit to Achill Island and no visit is complete without a trip to one or all of the five Blue Flag beaches that the island boasts. Check out Keem Bay on Achill's western edge, snugly nestled like a horseshoe between Moyteoge Head and the Croaghaun Mountain edge that spills into it, or Trawmore, which stretches for almost two miles at the foot of the Minaun Cliffs from Dookinella to Keel and is arguably the island's most majestic beach. Achill Seaweed Baths is another way to partake of the ocean's virtues during your visit.

Once you're tuckered out after a day of activity and sightseeing, there is no better place to restore your strength than at Patricia and Michael Joyce's Beehive Craft and Coffee Shop. Arrive for a pint of local craft beer and a hearty sandwich bursting with ingredients from the region and stay for the gift shop boasting artwork, clothing and stationery from local artisans.

OVER THE COURSE OF
THE PAST FEW DECADES,
HARDWORKING MUSSEL-
FARMING FAMILIES
HAVE CREATED A
TRADITION THAT NOT
ONLY SUSTAINS THEM
BUT INSTILS IN THEIR
COMMUNITY AN ABIDING
PRIDE THAT FORTIFIES
THEM EVEN DURING
TIMES OF STRUGGLE.

5 | Marty's Mussels

Catherine and Marty Nee

A love story began nearly three decades ago along the craggy western edge of the Irish coast. It was here that a British girl spied an Irish boy that her parents sternly warned her to stay away from. 'We holidayed in this area each summer and my parents told me that Marty was nothing but trouble,' recalls Catherine Nee with a smirk. 'That did it. I never forgot him.' She's an energetic blonde, with a proper British accent that stands out amongst the decidedly Irish inflections surrounding her.

'A few decades later, I had a fancy job in advertising and had just relocated to Paris when our paths crossed once more. Marty was so handsome, so charming,' she says with a wistful sigh. 'There was no getting around it. He won me over right then and there.'

After their brave attempt at a long-distance relationship finally ended when a baby was on the way, Catherine traded in her lavish lifestyle for a pair of waders and a fishing boat commanded by her stoic husband, Marty. He is soft-spoken and reserved, but his clear blue eyes speak volumes each time he glances over at his wife with an affection undiminished by time or the challenges of raising four children in the midst of running a successful mussel-farming business.

'Sometimes the problems seem to outweigh the rewards,' Catherine says in her matter-of-fact way over a steaming bowl of her family's own mussels that she enjoys in a corner booth in Paddy Coyne's Pub. 'But then I get out on the boat with Marty and we start harvesting our mussels. It feels so rewarding to own a business that supplies mussel lovers all over Ireland and the rest of Europe with a pristine product that I am so proud of.'

Catherine should be proud. Together with Marty, she has encouraged other families along the bay to take up the practice of mussel farming. Over the course of the past few decades, these hardworking families have created a tradition that not only sustains them but instils in their community an abiding pride that fortifies them even during times of struggle.

Mussel farming is a relatively new practice in the West of Ireland, even though its global origins are credited to a Connemara man who inadvertently began mussel farming in La Rochelle, France, in the thirteenth century. It was there that Patrick Walton from Galway noticed mussels breeding on the wooden poles he had plunged into the seabed in an attempt to catch birds, and it's gratifying for the residents of north Connemara, including Catherine and Marty Nee, that today the tradition is embraced in Killary Harbour. It might be a long way from La Rochelle but for Catherine Nee, a love-struck teenager from Britain turned Irish mussel farmer, it's the only place she could ever imagine calling home.

SMOKED BACON AND MUSSEL CHOWDER WITH CORN AND LEMON CREAM

This chowder is the perfect way to counter a blustery autumn day, preferably enjoyed beside a roaring fire surrounded by good friends. The smoked bacon pairs so well with the saline hint of the mussels and the sweetness of the corn and the lemon cream does a commendable job of brightening it all up with a velvety spoonful of spunk and vigour. If fresh corn is not in season, substitute with 400 g of tinned or frozen corn.

SERVES 4
PREPARATION TIME: 35 MINUTES

For the smoked bacon and mussel chowder with corn:

1 tbsp olive oil
4 smoked bacon rashers
1 medium onion, roughly chopped
2 celery stalks, roughly chopped
2 cloves garlic, finely chopped
800 ml chicken, fish or vegetable stock
2 large potatoes, peeled and roughly chopped
kernels from 5 corn on the cob
2 tsp ground cumin
1 tsp red chilli powder
salt and freshly ground black pepper, to taste
200 g mussels, shelled
zest of ½ lemon
500 ml double cream

For the lemon cream:
120 g sour cream
1 tbsp freshly squeezed lemon juice

To serve:
parsley, roughly chopped
sourdough bread

Heat the oil in a large saucepan over a medium heat. Sauté the bacon until crispy and slightly brown. Remove from the pan with a slotted spoon and drain on kitchen paper. Roughly chop it once it is cool enough to handle. In the residual bacon fat, sauté the onions, celery and garlic until the celery is tender but not brown, for about four minutes. Add the stock and stir up any brown bits on the bottom of the pan before adding the potatoes, half of the corn, cumin and chilli powder. Bring to a lazy simmer, reduce the heat to low and cook until the potatoes are fork tender, for about 12 minutes. As it cooks, whisk together the sour cream and lemon juice and refrigerate until ready to serve.

After removing the soup from the heat, use a handheld blender, taking great care to prevent the hot liquid from splattering, to blitz until smooth.

Season with salt and pepper, then return to the heat and add the cooked bacon, mussels, remaining corn, lemon zest and double cream. Cook until the mussels and cream are warmed through. Divide the chowder into bowls, dollop with lemon cream and garnish with parsley. Serve with crusty sourdough bread.

RENVYLE STEAMED MUSSELS

Paddy Coyne's Pub in Tullycross on the Renvyle Peninsula is the place to be in early May to celebrate the Connemara Mussel Festival. The event was conjured up a decade ago by Catherine and Marty Nee of Marty's Mussels and a few of their friends beside a peat fire in this very pub. The event is a celebration of the mussel-farming tradition that sustains many of the families in this region and Paddy Coyne's Pub is its sea-kissed heart. During the festival, the pub's chef dishes up steaming piles of mussels bobbing in a rich tomato cream sauce in its outdoor beer garden. There's nothing like plucking a plump, ocean-fresh mussel from its shell, washing it down with a swig of local pale ale and sopping up the residual juices with a hunk of tangy Irish soda bread. This recipe was inspired by that experience. It's such a shame that it doesn't come with a side of Paddy Coyne's craic.

SERVES 4
PREPARATION TIME: 30 MINUTES

800 g mussels
2 tbsp butter
1 medium onion, finely chopped
2 cloves garlic, finely chopped
4 plum tomatoes, roughly chopped
2 tbsp freshly squeezed lemon juice
2 sprigs thyme
400 ml double cream
2 tbsp sherry or brandy, optional
leaves from 4 sprigs parsley, roughly
    chopped
salt and freshly ground black pepper, to
    taste

To serve:
Irish soda bread (recipe page 108)
lemon wedges

Rinse the mussels under cold, running water to remove any residue, then trim away any fibrous beards. Place any of them that are slightly open on a counter and give them a gentle tap. If they close up, they're suitable for consumption. Discard any that remain open.

In a large cast-iron skillet or a heavy-bottom saucepan, melt the butter and sauté the onions, garlic and tomatoes over a medium-high heat until the onions are translucent and the tomatoes have broken down, for about four minutes. Add the lemon juice and scrape up any brown bits from the bottom of the pan. Add the thyme and mussels and continue to cook until the mussels have opened, for about four minutes more. Stir gently a few times during this process to marry the mussels with the cooking juices.

Once all of the mussels are opened, pour in the cream, splash with sherry and sprinkle with parsley. Season with salt and pepper. Continue to cook for one more minute or until the cream is warmed through, stirring once or twice to distribute the juices.

Divide the mussels and cream between four bowls. Serve with large hunks of soda bread, lemon wedges and, to set a festive mood, pints of ale.

BAKED WHITE FISH WITH BLACK OLIVES AND ROASTED TOMATO SAUCE

Salmon is perhaps the best-known fish captured along Irish shores, but its waters also teem with hearty white fish like cod, hake, pollock and haddock, all of which would work well in this recipe, as would halibut or sole. This is a nutritious yet simple dish to serve on a busy weeknight when there's the need to brighten up a winter chill with a few flavour notes from the Mediterranean. Serve over rice or a pasta variety that can catch the sauce, such as rigatoni or fusilli.

SERVES 4
PREPARATION TIME: 45 MINUTES

2 red peppers, seeded and sliced
  lengthwise into wedges
1 large red onion, sliced into wedges
6 plum tomatoes, sliced lengthwise
olive oil, as needed
salt and freshly ground black pepper, to
  taste
1 x 400 g tin chopped tomatoes
leaves of 6 sprigs parsley, roughly
  chopped
75 g pitted black olives
4 x 200 g skinless, boneless white fish
  fillets, such as cod, halibut or haddock
pine nuts or almonds, toasted

Preheat the oven to 220°C. Arrange the peppers, onion and tomatoes in a casserole, drizzle with olive oil and season with salt and pepper. Roast until aromatic and the edges are slightly charred, for about 20 minutes. Add the chopped tomatoes, parsley and olives and stir to combine. Season the fish fillets with salt and pepper. Arrange the fish in the casserole and cook until the fillets are cooked through, for about 18 minutes. Sprinkle with toasted pine nuts or almonds, if desired.

ELDERFLOWER BELLINI

The rose hue derived from the peach purée in a Bellini reminded the cocktail's inventor, Giuseppe Cipriani, the owner of Harry's Bar in Venice, of a Giovanni Bellini painting featuring saints draped in pink togas. The libation is traditionally comprised of peach purée topped off with a splash of sparkling wine, but in this recipe plum purée is paired with elderflower cordial for an Irish twist. As they do in much of Ireland, elder trees flourish in Connemara near the coast where Catherine and Marty harvest their mussels. The elder tree has always been venerated in Ireland, and was once considered so sacred that breaking a single twig from its branches was forbidden. At times it was associated with mischievousness and at others it was relied upon to ward off evil. The one thing that has remained constant through all of its incarnations is the captivating aroma and enchanting flavour of its blossoms, which are celebrated in this cocktail, ideal for a summertime garden party.

MAKES 1 BELLINI
PREPARATION TIME: 5 MINUTES

60 ml elderflower cordial
2 plums, peeled, pitted and puréed
sparkling wine, as needed
lemon wedges

Combine the cordial and plum purée in a cocktail shaker and shake vigorously to combine. Pour into a Champagne flute and top with sparkling wine. Garnish with a lemon wedge.

SEARED SCALLOP AND SUGAR SNAP PEA LINGUINE WITH ROCKET AND BROWN BUTTER SAUCE

Another ocean treasure to be found along the Wild Atlantic Way are hand-dived scallops. They are coveted along the Irish coast where divers brave frigid temperatures to retrieve these briny treasures. It's an ancient tradition that chefs like Kevin Thornton, owner of Thornton's restaurant in the Fitzwilliam Hotel in Dublin, pride themselves on keeping alive. A few times each spring and winter, Thornton, a spry chef with red curly hair and an impish grin, ventures to the Connemara coast, dons a wetsuit and dives for his own scallops, sea urchins and seaweed. In this recipe, scallops are quickly seared over a high heat before being paired with sugar snap peas, peppery rocket and a brown butter sauce that infuses it with a subtle caramelised flavour.

SERVES 4
PREPARATION TIME: 25 MINUTES

450 g linguine
125 g butter
1 small onion, finely chopped
3 cloves garlic, finely chopped
125 g fresh sugar snap peas
60 g rocket
salt and freshly ground black pepper, to taste
12 large scallops, trimmed, rinsed and patted dry

To serve:
mint leaves, torn
lemon wedges

Bring a saucepan of salted water to a vigorous boil. Reduce the heat to medium, add the linguine and simmer until tender, for about eight minutes. As the linguine simmers, melt one tablespoon of butter in a sauté pan over a medium heat. Sauté the onions and one clove of garlic until the onions are translucent and the garlic is aromatic. Strain the linguine, return it to the saucepan and toss with the onions and garlic. Cover to keep warm.

In the same sauté pan over a medium-high heat, combine the remaining butter and garlic. Melt the butter and cook until the butter is an amber colour, for about six minutes. Skim as necessary during this process to remove any residual foam and stir every few minutes to prevent scorching. Pour the brown butter over the linguine, add the sugar snap peas and rocket and toss gently to combine. Season with salt and pepper. Return the cover to enable the rocket to wilt and the peas to warm through.

Season the scallops with salt and pepper. Bring a non-stick frying pan to nearly smoking over a high heat. Working quickly with tongs, sear the scallops on both sides until golden brown, for about 90 seconds per side. Spoon the linguine into a bowl and top with three scallops. Garnish with mint and lemon wedges.

Irish Soda Bread

Soda bread embodies the resiliency and creative thinking of the Irish people. Traditionally comprised of nothing more than baking soda, flour, salt and sour milk, it was a filling component to the humble meals that sustained farming families throughout rural Ireland. Because it was traditionally baked in a cast-iron pot or on a griddle over a turf fire, it earned the moniker griddle cake or griddle bread.

This revered bread, with its hard crust and dense interior laced with a subtle tanginess, is still a mainstay on the Irish table today, gracing meals with a staple as beloved for its unique flavour as for the nostalgic memories it evokes. It is a form of 'quick bread', in that it relies upon the instantaneous reaction of baking soda with the lactic acid in buttermilk as its leavening agent as opposed to the more languid properties of yeast to induce rising. In some parts of Ireland, buttermilk is replaced with yogurt or even stout beer. It's enjoyed hot from the oven, slathered in rich Irish butter, in both its unadulterated incarnation as well as when embellished with goodies such as raisins, chocolate nibs or toasted nuts.

" Yes: I am a dreamer. For a dreamer is one who can only find his way by moonlight, and his punishment is that he sees the dawn before the rest of the world. "

OSCAR WILDE

Connemara
TRAVEL GUIDE

The village of Renvyle clinging to the edge of the Twelve Bens, the rugged Connemara mountain range, welcomes visitors with a warm embrace of cosy pubs, quirky shops and friendly residents who pride themselves on a local culture that pivots upon the mussel farms of Killary Harbour. Scuba diving, kayaking and sea angling are favoured pursuits in the region and the inviting village of Letterfrack along the border of Connemara National Park, a hiker's paradise boasting the famed Twelve Bens, is just a few miles away. There are plenty of hiking opportunities in the park to suit nearly any skill level. There is nothing quite like ascending to the top of one of the mountains to take in the view of the surrounding region on a clear Irish day.

Majestic Kylemore Abbey is just around the bend and a bit further afield is the charming seaside town of Clifden, with its breath taking Sky Road, an unforgettable drive through soaring cliffs and crashing waves. The manor house of Ballynahinch is a lovely place to rest your head while exploring the region or to enjoy a pint by the warming fire before continuing on your journey. The village of Leenaun, close to the fjord of Killary Harbour, is a great place to indulge in a seaweed bath, do a little shopping and enjoy a pint and a fine meal in one of the village's charming pubs.

'I WAS INSPIRED TO
BEGIN BREWING MY OWN
BEER IN CONNEMARA
BECAUSE I WAS ALWAYS
ATTRACTED TO ITS
RUGGED BEAUTY AND
THE INDEPENDENT
SPIRIT THE PEOPLE HERE
EXUDE. I HOPE THAT
OUR BEER REFLECTS THE
LANDSCAPE AND THE
VITALITY OF THE PEOPLE
HERE.'

6 | Independent Brewing

Kevin O'Hara

K evin O'Hara was studying to be a marine scientist in Galway before forsaking his career in aquatics to open Independent Brewing in 2014. He now applies his science background to brewing pale ale, red ale, IPA, porter and whiskey stout aged for nine months in used whiskey barrels in a small microbrewery in Carraroe, a windswept swatch of land on the edge of the Twelve Bens, a range of mountains on the coast of western Ireland.

A native of nearby Spiddal, O'Hara says, 'I was inspired to begin brewing my own beer in Connemara because I was always attracted to its rugged beauty and the independent spirit the people here exude. I hope that our beer reflects the landscape and the vitality of the people here.'

The logo's coral design, inspired by Coral Beach just down the road from the microbrewery, is comprised of small pieces of maerl, which is the coraline algae that gives the Coral Beach shoreline its distinctive coral colour.

Small-batch brewing is a relatively new practice in Ireland since large beer companies had a virtual monopoly for decades on the nation's beer market. O'Hara says things are changing as a result of the recession. 'After the crash, people began to look at what was around them because it was less expensive than importing everything. They also started to appreciate more the efforts of Irish food producers and sought out and encouraged the creation of higher-quality products.'

Ireland's artisan beer market is not only providing consumers with a vast new selection of brews to choose from, it is also fostering in farmers an incentive to grow barley crops specifically for microbreweries. O'Hara says, 'It's exciting to think that we are driving a market and creating a niche for sustainably grown Irish grain. We source our barley from a family-run farm in Louth that has been growing barley for over 100 years. I like having a direct connection to our farmer and I think this relationship is reflected in our beer. People who enjoy beer are ready for craft brews that are more flavourful and nuanced than the beer that is produced by the large multinational breweries. Craft brewers are filling a niche that was ready to be filled and I'm happy to be a part of it. It's an exciting time to be a craft brewer in Ireland.'

RHUBARB AND STRAWBERRY MUFFINS WITH BROWN SUGAR GLAZE

Sour cream gives these muffins a silky texture and a little ginger makes them a little fiery. If you're looking for a bit more brightness, substitute orange juice for half of the milk and if you'd like your rhubarb a little sweeter, soak it in warm simple syrup, a combination of equal parts caster sugar and water that is simmered until the sugar dissolves, for an hour before incorporating it into this breakfast treat. The glaze is also lovely spread over cakes or even drizzled onto waffles garnished with strawberries, if you're really feeling indulgent.

MAKES 12 MUFFINS
PREPARATION TIME: 35 MINUTES

For the rhubarb and strawberry muffins:
2 large eggs, beaten
1 tbsp milk
125 g sour cream
115 g butter, melted
1 tsp vanilla essence
250 g plain flour
100 g caster sugar
1 tsp cinnamon
1 tsp ground ginger
1 tbsp baking powder
½ tsp baking soda
pinch of salt
85 g strawberries, roughly chopped
85 g rhubarb, finely chopped

For the brown sugar glaze:
125 g icing sugar
75 g brown sugar
1 tsp vanilla essence
2 tbsp butter, softened
2 tbsp milk

Preheat the oven to 200°C and line a muffin tin with tin foil or paper baking cups. In a bowl, whisk together the eggs, one tablespoon of milk, sour cream, melted butter and one teaspoon of vanilla essence until smooth. In a second larger bowl, sift together the flour, caster sugar, cinnamon, ground ginger, baking powder, baking soda and salt and then fold in the sour cream mixture until the batter is thick and just beginning to come together. Don't overmix or the muffins will lose some of their airiness as they bake. Stir in the strawberries and the rhubarb and then spoon the batter into the muffin cups. It should be just a little bit higher than the top of each cup but should not overflow.

Bake until a toothpick inserted into the centre of a muffin comes out clean and the surface bounces back to its original form when gently pressed, between 20 and 24 minutes. Let stand at room temperature for 10 minutes before removing them from the tin.

To make the glaze, stir together the icing sugar, brown sugar, vanilla essence and softened butter until uniform. Add one tablespoon of milk and whisk until incorporated, then add a bit more at a time until you achieve the desired consistency. Frost the muffins straight away because the glaze will begin to harden immediately after it is ready.

WILD GAME TERRINE

The western forests, skies and lakesides of Ireland flourish with wild game such as duck, quail, pheasant, rabbit and pigeon. This terrine is a wonderful way to capture the essence of wild game and to celebrate the longstanding Irish tradition of eating it. It's simple enough to prepare and just requires an overnight to set properly. It's always a special addition to a meal, a way to pay tribute to the abundant virtues of the Irish countryside and, best of all, it encourages those you cherish to linger with an Irish stout in hand and a blazing fire fuelling the merrymaking.

MAKES 1 TERRINE
PREPARATION TIME: 1 HOUR (PLUS 24 HOURS FOR THE TERRINE TO SET)

8 boneless rabbit loins, trimmed
4 boneless pheasant breasts
2 boneless duck breasts
8 boneless quail breasts
salt and freshly ground black pepper, to taste
1 tbsp butter
250 g wild mushrooms, such as ceps, chanterelles or morels, or a combination of all three
6 sprigs parsley, finely chopped
1 litre game or chicken stock, reduced by half
4 sheets gelatine, softened in cold water and excess water squeezed out
12 smoked bacon rashers, cooked

To serve:
watercress
hard-boiled eggs, sliced
mayonnaise
cornichons or capers
wholegrain mustard

Preheat the oven to 175°C. Season the game meat with salt and pepper and arrange in an even layer in a roasting tin or a baking tray and roast until medium-rare, for about 15 minutes. Be sure to not overcook or the terrine will be too dry. Reserve the cooking juices and cool the meat to room temperature.

Next, melt the butter in a sauté pan and sauté the mushrooms until just tender. Add the parsley and sauté for one minute more. Combine the reduced game stock and the reserved cooking juices in a saucepan and bring to a simmer. Remove from the heat, add the gelatine and stir until dissolved.

To make the terrine, line a terrine mould with cling film and then arrange the bacon in a uniform layer on the bottom of the mould, leaving the excess to hang over one side of the mould and then the other, alternating sides as you go. The bacon should cover the entire interior of the mould and hang over the edge in a uniform way to enable it to cover the entire terrine once it's filled.

Next, line the mould with half the game meat, then half the mushrooms, then the remaining game and then the remaining mushrooms. Spoon a bit of the gelatine liquid over each layer as you go. Try to keep the layers uniform as you work and spoon any excess liquid over the last layer. Press the top down with a spoon to compress everything together before folding the bacon over the top of the terrine. Be sure the terrine is not releasing excess liquid.

Finally, weigh the terrine down with a heavy weight that fits the top of the mould. In a pinch, cut out a piece of cardboard to fit the interior of the mould, cover it with tin foil and then weigh this down with a brick covered in tin foil. Refrigerate for at least 24 hours before serving. To serve, cut with a sharp knife that has been warmed to encourage uniform slices. Serve with watercress, sliced hard-boiled eggs, mayonnaise, capers or cornichons and a quality wholegrain mustard.

BEEF, STOUT AND WILD MUSHROOM PIE

Beef and Guinness pie is a ubiquitous menu headliner throughout Ireland, but with the emergence of independently owned craft breweries, it's not just about Guinness anymore. Try using your favourite craft porter or stout as the foundation for this recipe, its elixir really, and let the ingredients mingle in an unhurried fashion, developing flavours as they should be developed, with patience and tenderness. Feel free to omit the bread base if you prefer a little less dough, and if you're aiming for a more communal dish that encourages sharing and inspires enduring conversation, use one large round dish instead of individual ramekins. Either way, this pie tastes best when dolloped with sour cream and paired with the stout or porter that went into it. The pies freeze well so make a few extra. You never know when you'll be in need of company and this recipe is the perfect enticement.

MAKES 4 PIES
PREPARATION TIME: 3 HOURS

1 kg stewing beef, cut into 3 cm cubes
salt and freshly ground black pepper, to taste
30 g plain flour
1 tbsp vegetable oil
1 medium onion, roughly chopped
1 large carrot, roughly chopped
1 celery stalk, roughly chopped
2 pints of your favourite stout or porter
1 clove garlic, finely chopped
250 g wild mushrooms, roughly chopped
1 sprig thyme
1 bay leaf
1 x 400 g tin chopped tomatoes
1 egg, beaten
splash of milk
1 ready-made sheet puff pastry

Season the beef with salt and pepper, then combine with the flour in a plastic bag and give it a good shake until the beef is coated. Heat the oil in a heavy-bottom saucepan or casserole and sear the beef until golden brown on all sides, for about three minutes. Add the onions, carrots and celery and cook until the carrots are just tender, for about five minutes. Deglaze the saucepan with a splash of the stout, scraping up any brown bits on the bottom. Add the garlic and mushrooms and cook until the mushrooms are tender, for about four more minutes. Stir in the thyme, bay leaf, tomatoes and the remaining stout and bring to a boil. Reduce the heat to a low simmer and cook slowly until the sauce is thick and the stew takes on the colour of the stout, through and through. Season with salt and pepper and remove the bay leaf.

Preheat the oven to 190°C. Prepare an egg wash by mixing the egg and a splash of milk. Roll out the puff pastry on a floured surface to about 1 cm thick. Using the top of a 30 g ramekin, cut out four circles of pastry about 1 cm wider than the ramekin and then another four circles about 4 cm wider than the ramekin. Grease the ramekins and press a large circle into each one, making sure that there is about 1 cm excess at the top of each ramekin. Brush the excess with a little egg wash. Fill the ramekins with the stew and top with a small circle. Use a fork to seal the pastry layers together and brush the tops with egg wash. Bake until golden brown and the stew is bubbling, for about 40 to 50 minutes. Serve while still very hot accompanied by a glass of the stout used inside.

CRISPY DUCK BREASTS WITH CARAMELISED CELERIAC AND RED ONION JAM

Celeriac, that gnarled orb that always looks like a hot root veg mess before it's peeled down to its elegant white interior, never receives its due. In this recipe, it's slow-roasted to bring out its sweet virtues and encourage caramelisation. When paired with a medium-rare duck breast boasting a golden brown and crispy skin, it's sure to turn everyone at the table into a celeriac convert. Duck never seems to receive the attention it deserves either, making this duo ideal bedfellows. The red onion jam they're paired with is an ideal accompaniment with its candied flavour and syrupy texture. Make an extra-large batch to use as a sandwich spread the next day or to pair with steak. It will keep in the refrigerator for up to two weeks.

SERVES 4
PREPARATION TIME: 40 MINUTES

For the red onion jam:
1 tbsp olive oil
2 red onions, halved and thinly sliced
2 tbsp stout beer
2 tbsp balsamic vinegar
250 ml red wine
75 g brown sugar
leaves from 1 sprig thyme
salt and freshly ground black pepper, to taste

For the caramelised celeriac:
1 medium celeriac, peeled and cut into bite-size pieces
2 tbsp olive oil
salt and freshly ground black pepper, to taste

For the crispy duck breasts:
1 tbsp vegetable oil
2 cloves garlic, thinly sliced
4 duck breasts, fat cap intact
salt and freshly ground black pepper, to taste
sea salt

Heat one tablespoon of olive oil in a saucepan and sauté the onions over a medium-low heat until they are very tender and completely translucent, for about 10 to 12 minutes. Add the stout beer, balsamic vinegar, red wine, brown sugar and thyme and increase the heat to medium-high to bring to a vigorous boil. Reduce the heat to low and let it simmer in a slow, lazy way until thick and syrupy, for about one hour. Stir a few times during this process to evenly distribute the cooking liquid. Once the desired consistency is achieved, season with salt and pepper and cool to room temperature. If not serving immediately, store the onion jam in a covered container in the refrigerator for up to two weeks.

Preheat the oven to 190°C. In a bowl, toss together the celeriac and two tablespoons of olive oil until the cubes glisten. Season with salt and pepper and arrange on a tin foil-lined baking tray. Roast until the edges start to turn golden brown and the surfaces lose their gleaming patina and transform to matte, for about 25 to 30 minutes. Turn once during the roasting process for even browning.

While the celeriac is cooking, heat the vegetable oil in a sauté pan over a medium-high heat. Add the garlic and sauté until a deep golden brown. Remove the garlic slices with a spatula or slotted spoon and either use for a garnish or discard. Season the duck breasts with salt and pepper and using a very sharp paring knife, score the duck fat in even lines about 1 cm apart from top to bottom. Reduce the heat to medium and sauté the duck, fat side down, until the fat cap is golden brown and caramelised, for about six minutes. Turn over and cook for three more minutes. At this stage, the duck will be medium-rare so cook for a few minutes longer if you prefer it medium. Remove the duck and let rest on a rack, fat side down. Flip after a few minutes to enable even distribution of the juices.

Slice the breasts and serve on top of the celeriac with a side of red onion jam, a sprinkle of crunchy sea salt and a generous glass of red wine. Drizzle the cooking juices over the entire plate as a final decadent flourish.

CHOCOLATE STOUT AND SEA SALT ICE CREAM

This creamy ice cream is such an enjoyable way to celebrate your favourite craft beer, especially if it's a heady chocolate stout. Add a dash of cayenne pepper if you're looking for a little excitement and don't skip the sea salt, which perks this little bowl of wonder right up with its plucky saline crunch.

MAKES APPROXIMATELY 1 LITRE OF ICE CREAM
PREPARATION TIME: 12 HOURS (INCLUDING ENOUGH TIME TO FREEZE THE ICE CREAM)

240 ml milk
180 ml double cream
300 ml chocolate stout or your dark beer of preference
5 egg yolks
100 g caster sugar
1 tsp sea salt
pinch of cayenne pepper, optional

In a heavy-bottom saucepan, combine the milk, cream and stout and heat until hot over a medium heat. Keep your eye on it during this step because you do not want the milk to boil or even come to a simmer. In a bowl, whisk together the egg yolks and sugar. Temper the yolks by adding about two tablespoons of the hot liquid, then whisking to incorporate. This step is important as it prevents the yolks from curdling or cooking. Repeat this process a few more times and then add the yolk mixture to the remaining hot liquid.

Return the pan to the stove and cook over a medium heat while stirring constantly with a wooden spoon. Continue to stir until the liquid is thick and creamy and coats the back of the spoon in a clinging layer.

Next, strain through a sieve so the finished ice cream is smooth and velvety, then stir in the sea salt to add a briny crunch. Add a pinch of cayenne pepper if you would like your ice cream to have a fun little kick. Refrigerate until cool, then prepare in an ice cream machine according to the manufacturer's instructions. Freeze until solid and enjoy on its own or with a warm chocolate brownie or cookies – the possibilities are endless.

Irish Cider

It is estimated that the cider-making tradition in Ireland stretches back at least 2,000 years. Up until the early twentieth century, the Irish enjoyed cider with as much gusto as beer. Farmhouse ciders were crafted throughout the nation in the eighteenth and nineteenth centuries and monasteries also embraced the practice. As it did with so many beloved food traditions, the famine nearly decimated the custom of cider-making and the first and second world wars in the twentieth century dealt it another nearly fatal blow.

A few large multinational cider-making brands are ubiquitous today in pubs throughout the nation, but in recent years, craft cider makers are finding a foothold in the industry. They are encouraged by a population that has come to appreciate the effort, passion and quality ingredients that comprise a quality craft cider. Each pint of craft cider ordered is another endorsement of a reclaimed tradition that eschews an impersonal, one-note product in favour of a nuanced libation that reflects the culinary awakening Ireland is currently experiencing. Sláinte!

"If you have the words,
there's always a chance that you'll find the way."

SEAMUS HEANEY

Galway
TRAVEL GUIDE

Galway never stops buzzing, its infectious energy fuelled by locals and tourists alike who flock to its cobblestoned streets for the merrymaking spilling from its pub, restaurant and shop doors. There's always something new to discover in Galway, a market to explore and a new friend to meet. A promising place to start is Sheridans Cheesemongers beside St Nicholas's Church. There's a wine bar upstairs and on the main floor is one of Ireland's finest selections of cheese, sourced by Seamus Sheridan, one of the nation's most renowned cheesemongers. It's easy for a cheese lover to lose an entire afternoon tasting cheese, at Sheridans until they remember how much more there is to see. Just outside is Galway's weekend street market, which hums with the industry and creative endeavours of its craft and artisan food makers.

JP McMahon's restaurant Aniar is a lovely place to spend an evening enjoying a tasting menu comprised of locally sourced ingredients such as chicken from The Friendly Farmer and foraged items such as sea buckthorn. Enda McEvoy's Michelin-starred restaurant Loam features a seasonally inspired menu with such indulgences as pickled sloes, Connemara air-dried lamb and cuttlefish with dillisk and ham. The Pie Maker must be one of western Ireland's cosiest little restaurants, with a full menu of comfy, savoury and sweet pies waiting to be tucked into on a chilly rain-soaked afternoon.

There is so much to discover in Galway, but should you need time away from the hustle and bustle, there's no better place than Inishbofin, a short ferry ride from Cleggan in County Galway. Indulge in a spa treatment at Inishbofin House Hotel and Marine Spa or tuck into a platter of crab claws washed down with local cider after a day spent seal-watching and biking around the island at The Beach, Day's Bar and B&B.

'I LOVE MY WORK,
I LOVE MY GOATS AND
I LOVE THE TRADITION
WE HAVE STARTED HERE
ON THE ISLAND.'

7 | Aran Islands Goats' Cheese
(Cáis Gabhair Arann)

Gabriel Faherty

Gabriel Faherty, a cheerful man with windswept cheeks and an endearing nature, is a goat's cheesemaker on Inishmore, the largest of the Aran Islands, a short ferry ride from the western coast. Less than a decade ago, Gabriel mustered up the courage to bring 50 kid goats to Inishmore to start his company, Aran Islands Goats' Cheese, and nearly six years after they arrived, his goats were finally ready to produce the volume of milk Gabriel required to produce his cheese.

Gabriel's story is one of tenacity, big dreams, learning on the go and heart, but he doesn't take all the credit for his recent success. He is quick to share credit with his fellow islanders, many of whom were so supportive of his dream from the get-go that they helped him bottle-feed the goats for their around-the-clock required feedings after they arrived on the island.

Gabriel's wife had four children in the ensuing years and he laughs when he explains, 'Sometimes it was a human baby in one arm being bottle-fed and a goat in the other doing the same. This business venture is certainly a family affair and I think that might be why my children are as interested in goats as I am.' His children know each of their nearly 150 goats by name and dutifully watch over the goats throughout the day like they are tending to members of their own family, rounding them up from the fields to head home to the barn each night.

Gabriel produces a plain goat's cheese used by his mother-in-law, Catherine Concannon, chef and owner of Teach Nan Phaidí, which is one of the best restaurants on the island. A wonder of a woman who can seemingly bake a dozen cakes, tarts and scones all at the same time, she has championed Gabriel's cheese from the very beginning, serving it in all manner of recipes, from a goat's cheese and dulse tart with red onion marmalade to a goat's cheese salad with smoked mackerel. Gabriel also produces a goat's cheese flavoured with dulse that he sources from a seaweed harvester on the island.

Gabriel says, 'It was touch and go there for a while and sometimes I wondered if I had made the right decision, but I no longer have those doubts. I love my work, I love my goats and I love the tradition we have started here on the island. My children are just as passionate about it and it's very satisfying to think that they will one day take over this work from me and that it will be something that is done here on Inishmore for generations to come.'

SUNDRIED TOMATO AND GOAT'S CHEESE SCONES

The nuns of Connemara's Kylemore Abbey, a striking abbey with resplendent Victorian gardens on a picture-ready spot on the edge of Pollacapall Lough, are renowned for their chocolate-making and for their scones, which they sell in the abbey's wonderful bakery and restaurant. Scone-making has a long history at Kylemore Abbey and throughout Ireland, where these round, crumbly breakfast gems are made all the more delicious when paired with rich Irish butter. Scones are a versatile vehicle for all manner of ingredients, from savoury to sweet. In this recipe, they're studded with sundried tomatoes, oregano and tangy goat's cheese.

MAKES 8 SCONES
PREPARATION TIME: 35 MINUTES

450 g plain flour
1 tbsp baking powder
1 tsp salt
1 tbsp dried oregano
6 tbsp butter, chilled and cut into
  2 cm cubes
8 sundried tomatoes, roughly
  chopped
50 g goat's cheese
1 tbsp olive oil
100 ml milk
2 large eggs, beaten

Preheat the oven to 190°C. Line a baking tray with parchment paper. Sift together the flour, baking powder and salt in a large bowl. Stir in the oregano. Add the butter and, using your fingers and a little finesse, incorporate it into the dry ingredients until it resembles coarse sand. Do not press it together too tightly: you want the batter to be airy and light at this stage. Add the sundried tomatoes and goat's cheese and stir to distribute evenly. In a second bowl, whisk together the olive oil, milk and eggs, then add the liquid to the flour mix and stir until everything is moistened and incorporated. Do not overmix, as you want to encourage an airy scone to form as it bakes.

The mixture will be a little sticky, so transfer it to a floured surface and pat it out into an even layer, about 3 cm thick. Punch out discs using a round metal cutter or even the top of a cleaned tin can. Combine the leftover dough and repeat the process until you have eight scones. Transfer them to the baking tray and bake until cooked through and slightly golden brown on top, for about 25 minutes. Serve while still hot with butter or with a jar of black olive tapenade.

LICKETY-SPLIT HOMEMADE CHEESE

Farmer's cheese is so easy to make and it sounds so impressive to tell your guests that it's homemade that there's no reason not to make your own cheese. You only require a little milk, lemon juice (or distilled white vinegar for a more neutral flavour) and some patience to allow the curds to split from the whey in their own sweet lactic time. If you opt for a softer cheese, the result will be similar to ricotta, which makes an incredible lasagne stuffing, pizza spread or dessert when drizzled in honey and sprinkled with toasted almonds or pine nuts. If you wait a little longer, the result will be a firmer, sliceable cheese that's irresistible on sandwiches. Either way, don't discard the residual whey. It's an amazing meat tenderiser, making it an ideal marinade ingredient. It also adds brightness to grains such as barley and amaranth when they're soaked in whey instead of water. Go ahead! Channel your inner cheesemonger and make this cheese at home. After you do it once and discover how simple it is, you'll never look at that bottle of milk in your refrigerator with all its cheesy potential the same way again.

**MAKES APPROXIMATELY 600 G
OF CHEESE
PREPARATION TIME: 2-4 HOURS,
DEPENDING UPON YOUR DESIRED
CHEESE CONSISTENCY**

2 litres milk
freshly squeezed lemon juice, as needed
salt, to taste

Add the milk to a heavy-bottom saucepan with a cooking thermometer attached to the side and warm over a medium heat. Stir almost constantly but with a placid hand, during this step so as not to scorch the milk and prevent it from boiling. Once the temperature reaches 80°C, remove the milk from the heat and add the lemon juice one tablespoon at a time, every few minutes, and keep stirring gently until the separation begins to happen. This step is to separate the curds from the whey, and while it might not seem like anything is happening, it will happen all of a sudden – you can't miss it. At this point, pat yourself on the back, take the saucepan off the heat and step away for about 15 to 20 minutes to allow the full separation to work itself out on its own.

Line a colander with a triple layer of cheesecloth or a doubled-up clean tea towel if you don't have cheesecloth on hand, and pour in the cheese. Let the curds drain at room temperature for at least 20 minutes but for up to an hour, depending upon your desired consistency. Season with salt by gently stirring it in. If you would like your cheese to have a firmer consistency, gather up the edges of the cheesecloth, spin the cloth to bring it together at the top and squeeze hard to remove the residual whey. Let it drain in the colander in the cloth and top with a weight such as a plate weighed down with a few tins of food. Let the cheese firm up for a few hours, or less time depending upon your desired consistency. If you prefer softer cheese, skip the pressing step and use the drained curds as you would use ricotta. It's best when absolutely fresh, but it will keep for up to one week in a covered container in the refrigerator.

BLACK PUDDING AND GOAT'S CHEESE FRITTATA

A frittata is the perfect breakfast vehicle for all of your leftovers at the end of the week. If you happen to find some Irish black pudding in your fridge, skip the traditional Irish breakfast of black and white pudding, sausage, bacon, fried eggs, grilled tomatoes and mushrooms and a side of beans (in case you were still hungry) and head straight for this lighter alternative. Black pudding is a common ingredient throughout many parts of eastern and northern Europe and it's no different in Ireland. This tender sausage containing pork, suet and dried pig's blood is a supermarket staple. Along the western coast of Ireland, food artisans are championing its virtues and longstanding legacy on the Irish breakfast table by creating their own unique versions of this beloved morning staple, experimenting with new flavours and ingredients. In this recipe, it's fried for a few minutes to make it crispy and then paired with creamy goat's cheese, which fortifies it with tanginess.

MAKES 1 x 24 CM FRITTATA
PREPARATION TIME: 35 MINUTES

15 g butter
1 medium onion, roughly chopped
250 g black pudding, crumbled into bite-
  size pieces
1 clove garlic, finely chopped
2 sprigs parsley, finely chopped
250 g goat's cheese, crumbled
10 large eggs
3 tbsp milk
salt and freshly ground black pepper, to
  taste
baby spinach, optional

Preheat the oven to 200°C. Melt the butter in a 24 cm ovenproof frying pan and cook the onion over a medium heat until nearly translucent. Add the black pudding and garlic and sauté until the meat darkens and begins to crisp up along the edges. Remove from the heat and mix in the parsley and goat's cheese. Allow to cool for a few minutes before adding the eggs so the eggs do not cook before reaching the oven.

In a large bowl, beat the eggs, then whisk in the milk and season with salt and pepper. Pour the eggs into the pan and stir very gently for just a few seconds to combine. Place the pan in the oven and bake until the edges of the frittata are puffed and golden brown and the eggs at the centre have set, for about 25 minutes. Serve while still hot with your preferred condiments and a handful of baby spinach to add a few more greens to the start of your day.

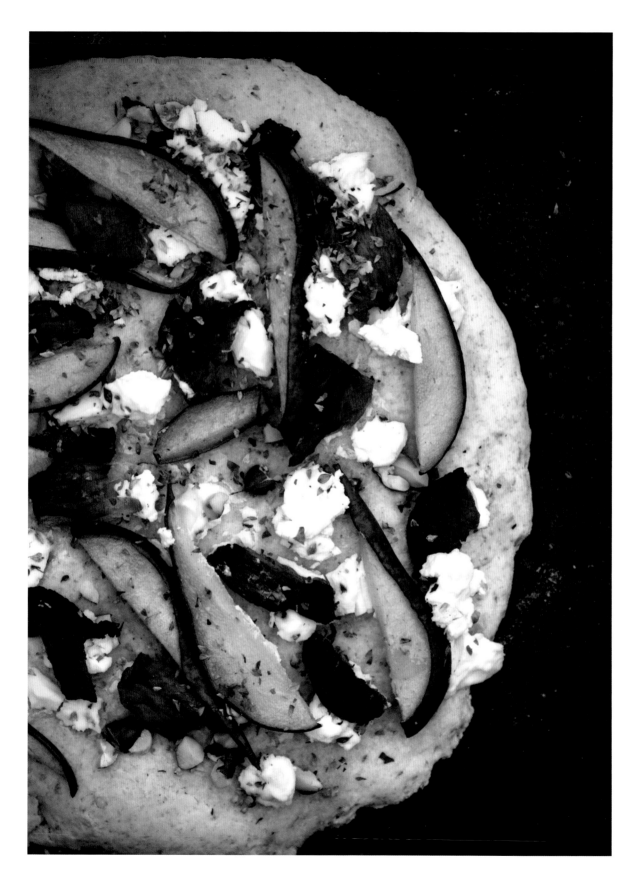

TOASTED HAZELNUT PIZZA WITH ROASTED PEARS, BACON AND GOAT'S CHEESE

This simple, no-yeast pizza dough is a lovely way to showcase roasted pears and crispy bacon that is mellowed by silky dabs of goat's cheese. Pressing hazelnuts into the dough before baking it gives this quick and easy weekend or busy weeknight dish an extra flourish of unexpected sophistication.

MAKES 1 PIZZA
PREPARATION TIME: 35 MINUTES

3 smoked bacon rashers
15 g butter
375 g plain flour
1 tbsp baking powder
1 tsp salt
2 tbsp olive oil
200 ml water, plus additional as
 necessary
3 tbsp hazelnuts, roughly chopped
2 pears, cored, halved and cut lengthwise
 into ½ cm segments
150 g goat's cheese, crumbled

Preheat the oven to 200°C. Sauté the bacon in butter, drain on kitchen paper, then cut into bite-size pieces. In a large, oiled bowl, sift together the flour, baking powder and salt. Add the olive oil and water and stir using a wooden spoon until a loose, shaggy ball forms. Add more water if you need to, but keep in mind that the texture should be on the dry, not sticky, side.

Transfer the dough to a clean, floured work surface and knead for four to five minutes to get the gluten working. Then transfer it to baking tray and flatten into your desired shape (circle, rectangle – any shape that takes your fancy), about 1 cm thick. Press the hazelnuts until they are semi-submerged into the dough and arrange the pears, bacon and goat's cheese on top. Bake until the dough is cooked through and the pears are roasted, for about 20 minutes. Slice and serve.

ROASTED CAULIFLOWER AND GOAT'S CHEESE RISOTTO

Risotto is not as fussy as you might assume and is well worth the patience required to coax the very best out of the plump Arborio rice kernels that comprise it. Risotto's trademark characteristic is its creaminess, and here that texture plays well with slow-roasted cauliflower and silky goat's cheese. Serve it as a side or as a main dish. Either way, your guests will think you fussed over it for hours when, in reality, it only demands 15 to 20 minutes of your undivided attention.

SERVES 4
PREPARATION TIME: 1 HOUR

400 g cauliflower
2 cloves garlic, finely sliced
1 tbsp olive oil
salt and freshly ground black pepper, to taste
1 tbsp vegetable oil
1 medium onion, finely chopped
450 g Arborio rice
100 ml white wine
400 ml chicken or vegetable stock
45 g butter
100 g goat's cheese

Preheat the oven to 190°C. On a baking tray, arrange the cauliflower and garlic slices. Drizzle with olive oil and season with salt and pepper. Roast until the florets begin to char on the edges, for about 20 minutes. Once the cauliflower and garlic are cool enough to handle, roughly chop them and reserve.

In a saucepan, heat one tablespoon of vegetable oil over a medium heat and sauté the onion until translucent. Do not let it turn golden brown. Add the cauliflower and garlic and sauté for two more minutes. Next, add the rice and turn the heat up to medium-high while stirring constantly. After a minute or two, the rice kernels will start to become translucent along the edges. Don't panic! This is the desired result. Add the wine and continue to stir until all of the liquid has been absorbed. Reduce the heat to medium-low and add one ladle of stock. Continue to stir as the liquid slowly simmers and the rice absorbs it. Once the liquid has been completely absorbed by the rice, add another ladle of stock and repeat the process. Continue to do so until the rice is completely cooked but the kernels still have a slight spring to their step. Overall, this should take around 20 minutes. A little patience is required, but the results are so worth it. Remove the risotto from the heat and stir in the butter and goat's cheese and season with salt and pepper.

Irish Butter

Irish butter is coveted the world over for good reason. The cows that produce the rich milk that comprises its feed on succulent grasses enriched by the *terroir* of a nation that has always endorsed a free-range lifestyle for their animals.

Dæge, the root of the word for dairy, is an Old English term that means 'female servant', and is an apt moniker. Not so long ago, butter-making was one of the few things a woman could produce to sell for profit that would be entirely her own, and it has always been the case in Ireland that most of the dairy shops were owned and operated by a female proprietor.

The Irish so love their butter that there is even a butter museum in Cork. Never a nation to let anything go to waste, the Irish have also reserved a prominent place for buttermilk, the by-product of butter-making, in their culinary repertoire by adding it to such breakfast staples as brown bread, scones and soda bread.

"Every life is many days, day after day. We walk through ourselves, meeting robbers, ghosts, giants, old men, young men, wives, widows, brothers-in-loves. But always meeting ourselves."

JAMES JOYCE

Inishmore
TRAVEL GUIDE

Be prepared to embrace a more relaxed pace of life when you arrive on the island of Inishmore, the largest of the Aran Island chain. Biking is the preferred and most convenient mode of transportation on the island and it's a joy to cycle from vista to vista, stopping for a pint or a bite to eat along the way. There are bike rental companies right next to the ferry terminal.

The first thing you'll notice right away on your two-wheeled adventure are the stone walls that create the patchwork of electric green fields that comprise nearly the entire island. Their distinctive patterns are as dramatic as the island itself.

Tí Joe Watty's in Kilronan village, a short ride from the ferry terminal, is one of the oldest Aran Islands pubs, boasting roaring open fires, nightly traditional music sessions and a fine selection of local seafood. Teach Nan Phaidí, a few miles down the road, serves the best baked goods, sandwiches, salads and soups on the island and is adjacent to the Kilmurvey Craft Village where local artists sell their finely crafted products, such as woollen mittens, stencilled wall tapestries and jars of milled seaweed.

Next door to the village is the entrance to Dún Aonghasa, one of Ireland's most visited and dramatic tourist attractions. This ancient stone fort, which sits on top of 300-foot cliffs that plunge fiercely into the lashing Atlantic below, dates back at least 3,000 years and is one of the best-preserved stone forts of this era in Europe.

'WHEN SOMEONE
TASTES ONE OF OUR
OYSTERS AND THEY
IMMEDIATELY ASK FOR
ANOTHER, THAT'S
HOW WE KNOW WE'RE
DOING IT RIGHT.'

8 | Kelly Oysters

Michael Kelly and Family

Over 1,000 years ago, the ancient kings of Connacht were fond of the oysters harvested from Killeenaran, an inlet along Galway Bay. But time did not look with favour upon Ireland's native oysters and they lost ground to inland proteins such as mutton and beef.

Diarmuid Kelly, who runs Kelly Oysters with his brother and father, both named Michael, says, 'It's an old tradition in Ireland, but it is only recently that contemporary Irish have begun to appreciate it.' Yet the Kelly family's admiration for their native oysters has never waned in the 60 years since the elder Michael founded the company. Michael is also one of the co-founders of the world-renowned Galway Oyster Festival, held at the end of each September. Oyster lovers gather here from around the globe to savour thousands of oysters over three spectacular days.

The Kelly brothers will identify for visitors to the shores where they harvest both native Irish and farmed gigas oysters the notes of Connemara sandstone, Burren limestone and the wild herbs and grasses from the fields of nearby Athenry. These flavours are carried to the frigid Atlantic waters that filter the oysters twice per day by the Kilcolgan and Clarinbridge rivers, fortifying the oysters until they are ready to harvest. Kelly Oysters are coveted the world over and the family exports them to places as far away as Dubai.

But it wasn't always that way. It required decades of devotion to a product they are just as proud of today as they were decades ago when they had no reassurance that their efforts would equate to success. For the family, there's only one true way to measure it. 'When someone tastes one of our oysters and they immediately ask for another, that's how we know we're doing it right,' Diarmuid says, before cracking open another oyster.

SPICED PUMPKIN BISCUITS WITH HONEY BUTTER

There's nothing wrong with having oysters for breakfast, but if you decide to wait a bit longer to indulge in their briny goodness, these satisfying biscuits are an ideal way to fortify a day of oyster-tasting along the Clare coast. These plump biscuits rise and rise and rise in the oven as a result of a few folds in the dough during their preparation and they are sure to become an instant go-to staple on your autumn table once you've tried them. Spiced up with a few seasonal flavours along with some tender fresh pumpkin, this might just become your biscuit of choice no matter what time of year it is.

MAKES 16 BISCUITS
PREPARATION TIME: 25 MINUTES

For the spiced pumpkin biscuits:
250 g flour
2 tsp baking powder
½ tsp ground cloves
½ tsp allspice
1 tsp cinnamon
pinch of salt
70 g butter
50 ml orange juice
50 ml buttermilk
1 tbsp honey
400 g pumpkin, roughly chopped

For the honey butter:
2 tbsp honey
zest of ½ orange
1 tbsp cinnamon
70 g butter, softened

Preheat the oven to 200°C. Sift together in a large bowl the flour, baking powder, cloves, allspice, cinnamon and salt. Add the butter and using your hands, incorporate it in until the flour resembles coarse meal. In a second bowl, whisk together the orange juice, buttermilk and honey until combined, then stir in the pumpkin until it is broken into pieces. Whisk to blend it completely. Pour the pumpkin mixture into the flour mixture and stir until everything is incorporated. At this stage, the dough should be slightly moist but not sticky.

Flour a clean work surface and roll the dough out into a 2 cm-thick rectangle. Dust it with flour and fold the rectangle in half, Roll out again, into another 2 cm-thick rectangle, then dust with flour and fold in half. Repeat the process three more times in order to ensure an airy biscuit. On the fifth roll, leave the dough in a flat, 1.5 cm rectangle and punch out circles using a 9 cm round metal cutter. Arrange on a parchment-lined baking tray and bake until puffed and cooked through, for about 15 minutes.

While the biscuits bake, whisk together the honey, orange zest, cinnamon and softened butter until light and fluffy. Cool the biscuits on a wire rack for a few minutes before serving warm with the honey butter.

GALWAY MULE

This is a whimsical Irish twist on the traditional Moscow mule. Hats off to you if you can get your hands on the traditional copper mug a mule is served in, but even if not, this cocktail is just as fun when served in a tall glass.

MAKES 1 GALWAY MULE
PREPARATION TIME: 5 MINUTES

½ lime
2 tbsp Irish whiskey
45 ml ginger beer

Squeeze the lime into the mug and drop the spent lime in behind it. Add three or four ice cubes and pour the whiskey on top of them. Top with the ginger beer.

OYSTER FRITTERS WITH CAPER DIPPING SAUCE

These tasty fritters are a wonderful way to indulge in the many virtues of oysters in a fun and unexpected way. Ideal for a hot summer day with an icy pint of beer, they're easy enough to whip up in a jiffy and promise to deliver an afternoon of mirth and enjoyment. Use an ice cream scoop to deliver the batter to the bubbling oil for frying or, if you prefer a little more whimsy in your fritter shape, freestyle it with a spoon. Use smoked oysters as opposed to fresh for a deeper flavour and serve them with this creamy caper dipping sauce and a generous amount of lemon wedges. And don't forget the beer!

MAKES APPROXIMATELY 14 FRITTERS
PREPARATION TIME: 20 MINUTES

For the caper dipping sauce:
6 tbsp mayonnaise
1 shallot, finely chopped
2 tbsp capers, roughly chopped
1 tbsp freshly squeezed lemon juice
salt and freshly ground black pepper, to taste

For the oyster fritters:
vegetable oil, as needed
250 g plain flour
2 tsp baking powder
pinch of cayenne pepper
½ tsp salt
2 eggs, beaten
200 ml milk
40 ml light beer (lager or pale ale work well)
350 g fresh oysters, roughly chopped
1 shallot, finely chopped

To serve:
lemon wedges

Blend together the mayonnaise, shallot, capers and lemon juice and season with salt and pepper. Refrigerate until chilled.

Pour around 5 cm of vegetable oil into a cast-iron skillet or another heavy-bottom frying pan and heat to 185°C. In a large bowl, sift together the flour, baking powder, cayenne pepper and salt. In a smaller bowl, whisk together the eggs, milk and beer and pour it into the flour mixture. Stir until smooth (the batter will be very wet). Mix in the oysters and shallot until incorporated.

Using a spoon or an ice cream scoop, drop batter into the oil and fry until the fritter puffs slightly and rises to the surface, for about two minutes. Flip over and repeat on the other side. Work in batches in order to avoid overcrowding. Remove the fritters using a slotted spoon, drain a plate lined with kitchen paper and season with salt. Repeat with the rest of the batter. Serve hot from the fryer with lemon wedges and the caper dipping sauce alongside.

PANKO-CRUSTED CRAB CAKES WITH BLACKENED TOMATO SALSA

Irish crab, harvested from the island's frigid and pristine waters, is extraordinary. There's nothing more fun than cracking open a bowl of crab claws at an outdoor table on the western coast on a glorious summer day. These crab cakes are an easy alternative to a steaming bowl of Irish crab claws, and while they might not be as interactive as the claws, they're just as tasty, especially when paired with blackened tomato salsa.

MAKES 8 CRAB CAKES
PREPARATION TIME: 25 MINUTES

For the blackened tomato salsa:
20 cherry tomatoes
2 tbsp olive oil
salt and freshly ground black pepper, to taste
½ small red onion, finely chopped
1 small cucumber, roughly chopped
1 tbsp freshly squeezed lemon juice

For the panko-crusted crab cakes:
½ small red onion, finely chopped
1 small red or yellow pepper, seeded and finely chopped
1 celery stalk, thinly sliced
1 tsp garlic powder
1 tsp yellow mustard powder
pinch of cayenne pepper
2 tsp Worcestershire sauce
1 tbsp freshly squeezed lemon juice
50 g Tuc or Ritz crackers (or starchy cracker of preference), finely crushed
1 large egg
1 kg crab meat, picked free of shells
salt and freshly ground black pepper, to taste
300 g panko breadcrumbs
vegetable oil, as needed

To serve:
mayonnaise or tartare sauce
lemon wedges

Preheat the oven to 200°C. In a bowl, toss together the tomatoes and one tablespoon of olive oil until the tomatoes are glistening. Season with salt and pepper, arrange in an even layer on a tin foil-lined baking tray and roast until the tomatoes start to blacken, for about 18 minutes. Toss with the red onion, cucumber, remaining olive oil, lemon juice and chilli flakes. Season with salt and pepper and keep at room temperature until ready to use.

For the crab cakes, mix together the red onion, red or yellow pepper, celery, garlic powder, mustard powder, cayenne pepper, Worcestershire sauce, lemon juice, crushed crackers and egg and stir to combine. Gently stir in the crab meat and season with salt and pepper. Form into eight cakes. Place the panko breadcrumbs in a small bowl and dredge the cakes in the panko breadcrumbs until generously coated.

Next, heat about 2 cm oil in a cast-iron skillet or heavy-bottom frying pan and line a plate with kitchen paper. Place two or three cakes in the oil at a time using a spatula and fry until golden brown, for about two minutes. Flip over and repeat on the other side. Drain on the kitchen paper and season with salt. Serve with the blackened tomato salsa, some mayonnaise or tartare sauce and lemon wedges.

ROASTED OYSTERS WITH HORSERADISH REMOULADE AND SHALLOT MIGNONETTE

What could be better than swallowing a raw oyster freshly plucked from the rugged coast of County Clare? Nothing, really, but these roasted oysters come in at a close second. Serve them immediately, hot and briny from the oven, with plucky horseradish remoulade and a splash of shallot mignonette.

MAKE 16 OYSTERS
PREPARATION TIME: 20 MINUTES

For the horseradish remoulade:
1 tsp horseradish sauce
1 clove garlic, finely chopped
pinch of salt
1 egg yolk
2 tsp Dijon mustard
400 ml olive oil
Freshly squeezed lemon juice, to taste

For the shallot mignonette:
1 small shallot, finely chopped
1 tbsp red wine vinegar
freshly ground black pepper, to taste

For the roasted oysters:
16 large oysters in their shells

For the horseradish remoulade, use a mortar and pestle or the back of a spoon to smash together the horseradish, garlic and enough salt to form a paste. Stir together the egg yolk and mustard in a medium-sized bowl, then add the garlic paste and stir to incorporate. Add about one-third of the olive oil in a slow, steady stream and whisk vigorously to emulsify. Once it reaches this stage, add the rest of your oil in the same slow, steady stream, pausing frequently to ensure that the remoulade is thickening up properly. Once all of the oil has been incorporated, whisk in the lemon juice and season with additional salt, if desired.

In a small bowl, stir together the shallot, red wine vinegar and pepper and refrigerate in a covered container until chilled.

Preheat the oven to 250°C. Arrange the oysters in a roasting tin and fill the bottom of the pan with 1 cm of water. Roast the oysters in the oven until the oysters begin to open, for about eight minutes. Using tongs, arrange the oysters on a platter with bowls of the remoulade and mignonette alongside.

A Brief History of the Irish Oyster

There is evidence of oyster consumption in Ireland dating back 5,000 years. Since then, the oyster's popularity has ebbed and flowed as consistently as the icy tides that filter them. Oysters in Ireland, much like seaweed, were long considered food for the poor, an ingredient to be consumed when little else was available or when a family was going through hard times. During the famine years of the nineteenth century, the highly nutritious oyster, which is packed with protein, zinc and other valuable vitamins and minerals, kept many people alive.

Today, the Irish oyster is a delicacy coveted around the world, its saline flesh and sweet juices telling the story of the pristine Irish coastline from which it is harvested. The Galway Oyster Festival in September, one of Ireland's largest and most esteemed food festivals, pays tribute to the oyster during three days of fevered consumption. The Irish oyster has come a long way from its status as food for the destitute and the Irish take great pride in this mollusc that grows slowly and flavourfully along its picturesque shores.

"There is no love sincerer
than the love of food."

GEORGE BERNARD SHAW

Kerry
TRAVEL GUIDE

The question is what *not* to do County Kerry. There's so much to explore in the area, which is characterised by its staggering beauty and uncompromisingly wild nature. A stop at the Dingle Distillery is a must for anyone who prefers independently owned spirits to industrialised libations that lack any real sense of their origin. The Dingle Distillery was the first to distil artisan spirits in Ireland for over 100 years and their tenacity alone justifies the trip. Then take a spin on Slea Head Drive, a circular route around the Kerry coast that begins and ends in Dingle, for views to rival any other along the Wild Atlantic Way.

On the Ring of Kerry, a visit to Kenmare is essential in order to saunter slowly up and down its picturesque streets brimming with inviting shops and restaurants. Perhaps the best place to enjoy a meal full of locally sourced fare is Martin Hallissey's restaurant, Packie's. Next, it's time to hit the Ring Road. Inch Beach and Skellig Michael are two sights not to miss along this road that is as much about getting a little lost as it is about crossing any particular destination off your list. The Avoca Café at Moll's Gap is a must-visit destination for food lovers and an ideal place to warm up after a blustery day driving the Ring Road.

INGREDIENTS SUCH AS POPPY SEEDS FROM POLAND, PECAN PIE FROM TEXAS AND ELDERBERRIES AND SEAWEED FROM IRELAND FIND THEIR WAY INTO HAZEL MOUNTAIN CHOCOLATE'S TRUFFLES AND CHOCOLATE BARS.

Salted Honey & Apricot Truffle €1.50.

9 | Hazel Mountain Chocolate

John and Kasha Connolly

Hazel Mountain Chocolate, located on a windswept hilltop in the heart of County Clare, is Ireland's first stone-ground bean-to-bar chocolate company. Its owners, John and Kasha Connolly, are rightfully proud of their whimsical chocolate factory, shop and café located in the former home of John's grandparents and they offer regular tours and lessons in chocolate-making.

Kasha hails from Poland and Hazel Mountain Chocolate's head chocolatier, Ana Murphy, found her way to this remote corner of Ireland via Texas when she married a local man from Doolin, a village just down the road renowned for its traditional music. Ingredients such as poppy seeds from Poland, pecan pie from Texas and elderberries and seaweed from Ireland find their way into Hazel Mountain Chocolate's truffles and chocolate bars sold in the on-site shop, and the neighbouring café subtly includes cacao in savoury dishes, such as goat's cheese and potato dumplings with sage cacao butter.

Kasha says that she and her team are learning as they go and enjoy experimenting with local flavours and the traditions they each bring to their inviting chocolate-making table. Their beans, which arrive in massive burlap sacks from as far away as Cuba, Madagascar and Venezuela, are cracked, sifted and winnowed on-site before they are stone-ground for 40 hours, then tempered and transformed at long last into chocolate. Their milk chocolate bars are comprised of rich milk from Irish grass-fed cows and their dark chocolate features raw cane sugar, before finally being transformed into some of Ireland's finest truffles and chocolate bars, sold in one of the most remote bean-to-bar chocolate shops in the world.

'It's sometimes a challenge to explain how arduous the process can be to make bean-to-bar chocolate, how time-consuming it is and how much more challenging it is to begin with a raw bean instead of chocolate from a box that is tempered without involving any of the other steps,' Kasha says. She pauses to survey her inviting chocolate shop with its shelves brimming with the team's award-winning chocolate before continuing, 'But we wouldn't have it any other way and we accept the challenge. Usually we can overcome it once the visitor tastes our chocolate and discovers for themselves just how special it is.'

SMOKED TROUT AND BARLEY SALAD WITH LIME VINAIGRETTE

The café at Hazel Mountain Chocolate serves a revolving menu of salads that change with the seasons and the whimsy of the chef. This recipe is inspired by ingredients sourced from the Irish land and sea. Barley is an important crop in Irish agriculture and while it is often malted for beer-making, it's also enjoyed as a nutritious and welcome alternative to the standard side of potatoes. In this recipe, pearl barley is used, but feel free to use the wholegrain variety instead. It's paired with smoked trout, another Irish favourite, along with charred corn, lime vinaigrette and a smattering of toasted walnuts. Walnuts also appear in the vinaigrette in the form of walnut oil, but if you have trouble sourcing it, any nut oil or even olive oil are good substitutes. Fresh summer corn is preferred, but tinned or frozen corn will work too. The barley is prepared using chicken or vegetable stock, but feel free to use water for a lighter alternative.

SERVES 4
PREPARATION TIME: 1 HOUR

For the smoked trout and barley salad:
400 ml water
350 ml chicken or vegetable stock
125 g pearl barley
salt and freshly ground black pepper, to taste
125 g corn
16 cherry tomatoes, halved
250 g smoked trout fillet, torn into pieces
100 g walnuts, chopped and toasted

For the lime vinaigrette:
2 tbsp freshly squeezed lime juice
1 tsp Dijon mustard
2 tbsp walnut oil
salt and freshly ground pepper, to taste

To serve:
lime wedges

In a saucepan bring the water, stock and barley to a boil. Reduce the heat, cover and simmer until the barley has completely absorbed the liquid and is tender with only a hint of a bite, for about 55 minutes. Season with salt and pepper.

While the barley cooks, whisk together the lime juice, mustard and walnut oil until emulsified. Season with salt and pepper and keep at room temperature until the barley is ready.

Next, heat a dry, non-stick frying pan over a high heat and add the corn. Let it char on both sides for about three to four minutes. Toss together the barley, tomatoes, charred corn, smoked trout and toasted walnuts. Pour the vinaigrette over the top and stir gently until everything is glistening. Serve with lime wedges on the side.

ROSEHIP SYRUP

At Hazel Mountain Chocolate, the ingredients that flavour the chocolate are frequently foraged from the surrounding hillsides and hedgerows. Rosehips are a member of the apple family and in the early autumn they are to be discovered in abundance in the hedgerows of rural Ireland. These teardrop-shaped, ruby red gems are higher in vitamin C than oranges and they have been transformed for centuries into a syrup suitable for everything from pancakes and bread to waffles and scones. The only trick with this recipe is to be sure to simmer and drain them a few times to remove the prickly hairs that accompany these Celtic beauties.

MAKES APPROXIMATELY 1 LITRE OF SYRUP
PREPARATION TIME: 1 HOUR

700 g rosehips
3 litres water
caster sugar, as needed

Preheat the oven to 125°C. Wash a one litre swing-top vinegar bottle with warm soapy water and rinse well. Place in the oven until completely dry.

Chop the rosehips as finely as possible or pulse them in a food processor. Add the rosehips and half of the water to a saucepan and bring to a boil, then reduce the heat to low and simmer gently for 20 minutes. Next, place a double layer of cheesecloth or a single tea towel over a colander set inside a bowl and drain the rosehips for about 30 minutes. Reserve the juice and return the rosehips to the saucepan along with the rest of the water. Bring to a boil again, then reduce the heat to low and simmer gently for another 20 minutes. Strain as above into the reserved liquid. Prepare a fresh double-layer of cheesecloth and then strain the liquid once more to remove all of the irritating little rosehip hairs.

Wash the saucepan to remove any residual hairs, then measure the rosehip liquid and pour it back into the saucepan. For every 500 ml of liquid, add 300 g of sugar. Bring to a simmer over a medium heat and stir until the sugar dissolves. Increase the heat and boil for four minutes, skimming any scum that forms on the surface. Carefully pour the syrup into the sterilised vinegar bottle and seal it shut. The syrup will keep for up to three months and should be refrigerated once opened.

106 | RECIPES AND STORIES FROM IRELAND'S WILD ATLANTIC WAY

DOUBLE CHOCOLATE AND TOASTED OAT COOKIES

These double chocolate cookies are given a little unexpected twist with the addition of toasted oats, which infuse them with a gratifying chewiness. They are best served warm from the oven with a side of ice-cold milk.

MAKES 16 COOKIES
PREPARATION TIME: 20 MINUTES

100 g rolled oats
300 g flour
1 tsp baking powder
3 tsp cocoa
pinch of salt
200 g caster sugar
200 g butter, softened
2 eggs, beaten
1 tsp vanilla essence
200 g chocolate chips

Preheat the oven to 180°C. Arrange the oats in an even layer on a baking tray and toast until just golden brown, for about three minutes. In a large bowl, sift together the flour, baking powder, cocoa and salt. In a second bowl, using a handheld mixer, cream together the sugar and butter until light and fluffy, then add the eggs and vanilla essence and beat until thoroughly incorporated. Add half of the flour, only adding the second half after the first is completely incorporated. Stir in the chocolate chips and the toasted oats.

Each cookie should be about two tablespoons of batter. Spread them evenly on a baking tray. Bake for between 11 and 13 minutes. The cookies should be tender and soft when removed from the oven, but they will harden up as they cool down. Once completely cool, remove from the baking tray using a spatula and store in a covered container for up to one week.

IRISH SODA BREAD

The soda bread used in many of the sandwiches served at the Hazel Mountain Chocolate café is homemade and frequently arrives at the table still hot from the oven. Irish soda bread is one of the simplest and most pleasing bread recipes that has ever been concocted by a creative population with few resources. In this recipe, wholemeal flour is used, but feel free to substitute it with plain white flour for a lighter texture.

MAKES 1 LOAF OF BREAD
PREPARATION TIME: 1 HOUR

450 g coarse wholemeal flour
1 tsp baking soda
1 tsp salt
400 ml buttermilk

Preheat the oven to 220°C and grease a 1 lb bread tin. Sift the flour, baking soda and salt together into a large bowl, then add the buttermilk. Bring the dough loosely together either by using a wooden spoon or stirring by hand. On a floured work surface, gently knead the dough until it just begins to come together into a shaggy ball. Do not overwork it. Shape it into a loaf and place it in the bread tin; alternatively, shape it into a circle and place it on a greased or lined baking tray.

Bake for 30 minutes on the centre rack, rotating it 180° once during the baking process to ensure even browning. Once the surface is golden brown and a toothpick inserted in the centre comes out clean, let the tin sit at room temperature for five minutes before removing the bread and cooling it on a wire rack for an additional 30 minutes. Soda bread is best when eaten the same day, preferably slathered in creamy Irish butter.

CHOCOLATE POITÍN OLD FASHIONED

Poitín, or Irish moonshine, was traditionally made in small stills throughout the Irish countryside. Today poitín is having a moment, with artisan brands emerging throughout the nation. Here it is paired with chocolate liqueur in an Irish-inspired Old Fashioned. Of course, if you don't have access to poitín, your favourite Irish whiskey is a good substitute, but let's face it, the nefarious legacy that poitín carries with it is so much more fun to swirl into the glass.

MAKES 1 OLD FASHIONED
PREPARATION TIME: 5 MINUTES

1 tsp simple syrup
2 dashes Angustora bitters
1 euro coin-size orange peel
  (including the pith)
1 tbsp chocolate liqueur
2 tbsp poitín

In a small tumbler, combine the simple syrup, which is a combination of equal parts water and caster sugar brought to a boil and simmered until the sugar is dissolved, with the Angustora bitters, then fill the glass halfway with ice and stir for 30 seconds. Squeeze the orange peel over the ice to release its oil and then drop the peel into the glass. Add the chocolate liqueur and the poitín, add enough ice to fill the glass to the top and stir for another 30 seconds.

Rigney's Farm

There's an ancient fairy fort, with a tire swing in the middle of it, on the property line of Rigney's Farm, a B&B and working family farm raising rare breed animals near Limerick in south-western Ireland. 'The cows come here to give birth. I suppose it's because it's flat in the centre beyond the stone ring, but I also like to think there's some energy at work from the past that brings them to what I like to call the farm's maternity wing,' says co-owner Caroline Rigney, who frequently serves her arriving guests freshly baked scones hot from her oven and slathered in homemade butter. She is also the founder of Curraghchase Meats, a company she set up to sell the dry-cured ham, homemade black and white puddings and other products derived from the farm's animals, such as her beloved Tamworth and Saddleback pigs and white and brown speckled Jacob sheep, at a local famer's market.

When Caroline isn't processing meat, working a local farmer's market or accompanying her guests to the barn to gather their own eggs for breakfast, she's surveying the wild grass field behind the house to assess if it's ready to be harvested for hay by her husband, Joe, a former stone mason who lovingly crafted the impressive stonework throughout the property that the couple built from 'nothing but green field'.

Caroline says she wants to provide her guests with a traditional pastoral experience, but says, 'I didn't grow up on a farm, but because of this, I had a romantic vision of what farming should be. Maybe it's better that I didn't have any experience when we started because I was then able to shape my vision into my reality.'

'I DIDN'T GROW UP ON A FARM BUT BECAUSE OF THIS, I HAD A ROMANTIC VISION OF WHAT FARMING SHOULD BE. MAYBE IT'S BETTER THAT I DIDN'T HAVE ANY EXPERIENCE WHEN WE STARTED BECAUSE I WAS THEN ABLE TO SHAPE MY VISION INTO MY REALITY.'

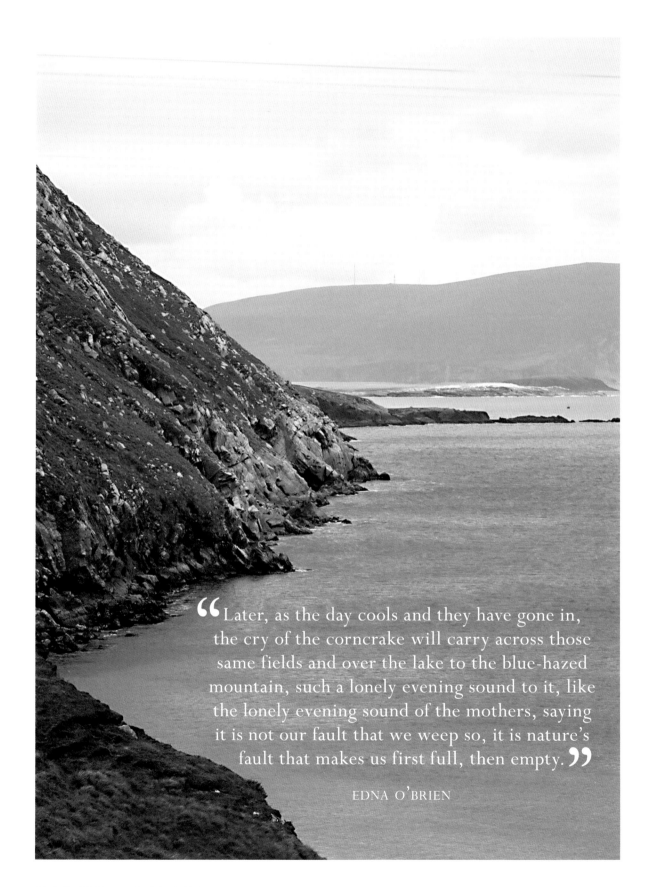

"Later, as the day cools and they have gone in, the cry of the corncrake will carry across those same fields and over the lake to the blue-hazed mountain, such a lonely evening sound to it, like the lonely evening sound of the mothers, saying it is not our fault that we weep so, it is nature's fault that makes us first full, then empty."

EDNA O'BRIEN

Clare
TRAVEL GUIDE

There is so much to explore along the coast in County Clare that the best thing to do is hop in your car and start driving. Kinvara is the gateway village to the coast of Clare, and what a gateway it is, with captivating Dunguaire Castle at its entrance.

While exploring the surreal limestone landscape of the Burren, make sure to stop by the famed Cliffs of Moher to take in their unrivalled beauty. Be sure to poke your head into a pub in Doolin to catch a trad session after fortifying yourself at the Roadford House Restaurant, which offers such delicacies on their menu as whiskey and mustard-cured salmon and chicken liver and foie gras with cider-soaked raisins and date jam.

In Lahinch, meander along the beach to watch the surfers glide along the riot of waves or rent a board yourself and give it a whirl. Angling, canoeing and scuba diving are other ways to scratch your outdoor itch during your visit to this stretch of coast.

In Lisdoonvarna, don't miss a craft beer at the Roadside Tavern, one of Ireland's finest microbreweries, where the owner, Peter Curtin, will tell you tales of his struggles and triumphs in his ongoing quest to stay relevant as a traditional Irish pub. His most recent solution was to open the Burren Brewery within the pub in order to brew his own beer in the hope of carving out a unique niche for himself. It's working and it's well worth a stop for both a pint and a spirited conversation with Mr Curtin himself.

Once you're through with your pint, he'll send you down the road to the Burren Smokehouse, which is owned by his wife, Birgitta Curtin, a native of Sweden who employs both hot and cold smoking techniques derived from her native country and her adopted home. The shop also sells a fine selection of local food products in its storefront, where smoked salmon tastings are as much an education as they are an afternoon indulgence.

WEST CORK HAS
ALWAYS BEEN AN
EXTRAORDINARY
PLACE FOR ARTISAN
FOOD PRODUCERS
BECAUSE THERE IS AN
ENVIRONMENT HERE
THAT PROVIDES A
SUPPORT NETWORK
AND ENCOURAGES
CREATIVITY AND FREE
THINKING.

10 | Gubbeen Farm

Fingal Ferguson and Family

The Gubbeen farm near the village of Schull in West Cork has stood on the edge of the sea for six generations, each one employing the traditional practices of their ancestors to ensure that when it is time, a self-sustaining farm is delivered to the next stewards of this fertile land.

The current caretakers of Gubbeen farm include husband and wife Tom and Giana Ferguson and their children, Fingal and Clovisse. Each is respected by the others for their talents and encouraged to indulge in their passions, transforming a traditional family farm into a visionary business that serves as a template for farmers everywhere.

Clovisse nurtures biodynamic fields of chemical-free vegetables, herbs and fruits fertilised with seaweed, while her mother, Giana, tends to the poultry and cultivates her pioneering cheese programme which introduced some of the first artisan cheese to the nation. Fingal oversees the pigs from which he produces a vast selection of pork products, including Ireland's first chorizo, while crafting enviable knives coveted by chefs throughout the country. Tom ensures that the farming customs of his ancestors are preserved by cultivating the land using their time-honoured practices.

Fingal says, 'West Cork has always been an extraordinary place for artisan food producers because there is an environment here that provides a support network and encourages creativity and free thinking. I feel so fortunate to have grown up here amongst so many inspiring people who taught me not only how to follow my passions, but to trust my instincts and indulge in my curiosities too.'

Each member of the Ferguson family occupies their own special niche, but they collectively adhere to the ethos of 'value-added food production', a philosophy ensuring that when it's time for Gubbeen farm to transfer hands once more, it will be more vital and hold more promise than it ever has before.

WEST CORK PORRIDGE WITH MAPLE SYRUP AND TOASTED PECANS

Kilbeggan Organic Foods in West Cork produces one of Ireland's best porridges, comprised of hearty oats that are grown slowly in the long but temperate Irish summer. Here the porridge is served with a drizzle of maple syrup and crunchy toasted pecans, but a few other ideas for a healthy morning start include bananas and cinnamon, roasted apples, summer berries, shaved coconut or toasted pumpkin seeds. Soy or almond milk are easy alternatives for the milk. No matter how you serve this comforting blank canvas, be sure to use the very best oats you can find.

SERVES 4
PREPARATION TIME: 10 MINUTES

175 g rolled oats
550 ml milk
salt, to taste
maple syrup
pecans, toasted

Combine the oats and milk in a saucepan and bring to a rolling simmer over a medium heat. Season with salt and stir with a wooden spoon until thick and creamy, for about five minutes. If you would like a looser porridge, add a bit more milk at the end of the cooking process. Spoon into a bowl, drizzle with maple syrup and sprinkle with toasted pecans.

SMOKED SALMON DIP

Smoked salmon is synonymous with western Ireland, where it is smoked using longstanding traditional methods from the northern tip of the coast to its very southern edge. In this recipe, it's incorporated into an addictive dip that's made all the better when served with snappy crackers, slices of thinly sliced and toasted rye bread or raw vegetables such as carrots, cucumbers or cauliflower.

MAKES APPROXIMATELY 250 G OF DIP
PREPARATION TIME: 10 MINUTES

50 g cream cheese
25 g sour cream
1 tsp freshly squeezed lemon juice, plus additional for seasoning
1 tbsp capers
1 tbsp horseradish sauce
1 tbsp finely chopped shallot
115 g smoked salmon
leaves from 1 sprig dill
salt and freshly ground black pepper, to taste
crackers, rye bread or raw vegetables

In the bowl of a food processor, combine the cream cheese, sour cream, lemon juice, capers, horseradish, shallot and half of the salmon and blend at high speed until smooth. Transfer to a serving bowl and stir in the remaining salmon and the dill. Season with additional lemon juice, if desired, along with salt and pepper. Serve with crackers, rye bread or raw vegetables on the side.

GRILLED PRAWN AND SMOKED SAUSAGE SALAD WITH PICKLED LEMON CUCUMBERS

This is a lively summertime recipe featuring grilled prawns, smoky sausage, chickpeas and quickly pickled lemon cucumbers. The excellent chorizo from Gubbeen Smokehouse is the recommended sausage of choice, but if you're not fortunate enough to live in Ireland, where it is available in all corners of the country, any quality smoked sausage will do. Add a handful of spicy sunflower seeds for a little extra heat or omit the chilli altogether and toast up the seeds unadulterated.

SERVES 4
PREPARATION TIME: 20 MINUTES

For the pickled lemon cucumbers:
1 cucumber, halved lengthwise and sliced
zest of 1 lemon
250 ml water
2 tbsp freshly squeezed lemon juice
2 tbsp apple cider vinegar
50 g caster sugar

For the grilled prawn and smoked sausage salad:
1 tbsp vegetable oil
2 large smoked sausages, such as chorizo or andouille
24 unshelled prawns
3 tbsp sunflower seeds
½ tsp red chilli powder, optional
400 g chickpeas
4 sprigs parsley, roughly chopped
2 tbsp olive oil
chives, coarsely roughly
salt and freshly ground black pepper, to taste

Place the cucumbers and lemon zest in a heatproof bowl. In a saucepan, bring the water, lemon juice and apple cider vinegar to a boil. Remove from the heat, add the sugar and stir until dissolved. Pour the hot liquid over the cucumbers and cool to room temperature. Drain if ready to use or refrigerate in a covered container for up to one week.

Heat the vegetable oil in a sauté pan and fry the sausages until charred and cooked through. Once they are cool enough to handle, slice into bite-size pieces. Heat a cast-iron skillet or heavy-bottom frying pan over a high heat to nearly smoking. Using tongs and working quickly, grill the prawns until pink and seared on both sides, for about one minute per side. Once they are cool enough to handle, peel, discarding the shell. Devein if desired. Toss together the sunflower seeds and the red chilli powder and toast in a clean, dry pan until golden brown, for about one minute.

In a large bowl, toss together the cucumbers, sausage, prawns, sunflower seeds, chickpeas, parsley and olive oil until everything is well coated. Season with salt and pepper and garnish with chives. Divide into four bowls and serve on a summer's day with an ice-cold beer.

SLOW-ROASTED PORK TENDERLOIN WITH LENTILS AND KALE

This is a nice alternative to the traditional Sunday roast, and even though it looks elegant and complicated on the platter, it's a relatively easy dish to pull together. Feel free to substitute Swiss chard for the kale, but nothing will substitute for wholegrain mustard, which adds a pleasant zing to this dish.

SERVES 4
PREPARATION TIME: 1 ½ HOURS (PLUS 12 HOURS' SOAKING TIME FOR THE LENTILS)

For the lentils and kale:
100 g red lentils
500 ml water
1 bay leaf
1 clove garlic, thinly sliced
200 g torn kale leaves, stemmed
salt and freshly ground black pepper, to taste

For the roasted pork tenderloin:
1 pork tenderloin
salt and freshly ground black pepper, to taste
1 tbsp vegetable oil
1 medium onion, halved and thinly sliced
250 ml chicken or vegetable stock
1 tbsp wholegrain mustard

Prepare the lentils by soaking them in water overnight. Preheat the oven to 200°C. Drain the lentils and transfer to a saucepan along with the water, bay leaf and garlic. Bring to a boil, then reduce the heat to medium-low, cover and cook until tender, for about 30 minutes. Discard the bay leaf and reserve the lentils in their cooking juices.

Season the pork tenderloin with salt and pepper. In an ovenproof sauté pan, heat the oil over a high heat and sear the pork on both sides until golden brown. Transfer to a plate and reserve. Add the onion to the pan and sauté until translucent. Add the stock and mustard to the pan and bring to a boil. Return the loin to the pan and put the entire pan in the oven, roasting the pork until a thermometer reads 65°C. Remove the pan from the oven and using tongs, transfer the loin to a rack to rest.

Add the lentils and their cooking juices along with the kale to the sauté pan and stir to combine everything. Season with salt and pepper. Bring the lentils and kale to a simmer over a medium heat, for about 45 minutes. Then, when you're ready to serve, slice the pork tenderloin, pour the lentil mixture onto a platter and place the pork slices on top.

HOME KITCHEN DINGLE CLAM BAKE

You don't need a beach to enjoy a clam bake, but you do need quality seafood and sausage to really make it work. The ideal ingredients would be sourced from the ocean licking western Ireland's shores and the Gubbeen Smokehouse, but as long as you have access to fresh seafood, you can whip this fun but simple party-in-a-pot up anywhere, even in your own home kitchen. The key is to heat the liquid inside enough to steam the shellfish open. If it's raining outside, bring the summertime beach inside by spreading out newspapers on your dining room table and encouraging a mess in the form of flying seashells.

SERVES 4 TO 6
PREPARATION TIME: 1 HOUR

2 tbsp olive oil
1 medium onion, coarsely chopped
2 large Rooster or white potatoes, peeled
salt and freshly ground black pepper, to taste
300 g chorizo
400 g clams
400 g prawns
400 g mussels
2 lobsters
800 ml white wine

To serve:
prawn crackers
lemon wedges

Heat the olive oil in a large heavy-bottom saucepan and sauté the onions over a medium heat until nearly caramelised, for about 12 minutes. Layer the potatoes over the onions and season with salt and pepper. Next, add a layer of chorizo, then one of clams, then prawns and then mussels. Finally, add the lobsters and pour the white wine over everything. Cover, turn the heat up to high and cook for 10 minutes or until steam begins to escape from the seal of the lid. Reduce the heat to medium and cook for another 20 minutes. Everything should be ready: the mussels and clam shells should be open and the prawns and lobster meat should be pink.

Line a table with newspapers and lay a bowl or deep platter large enough to accommodate everything, including the cooking juices, in the centre of the table. Fill it with the potatoes, chorizo, mussels, clams and prawns, then top it with the lobsters for dramatic effect and pour the onions and cooking liquid on top, being careful not to include the residue at the bottom of the saucepan. Place some prawn crackers on the table along with lemon wedges and rolls of kitchen paper. Dig in and celebrate the season and the sea!

Fish Smoking

When you're the wife of a fisherman in West Cork, a region in the far south of Ireland renowned for its food artisans, it makes sense to open a fish-smoking business that serves as 'the land-based side of the operation', says Sally Fernes Barnes, a native of Scotland who first started smoking fish in a converted tea chest.

In 1981 she opened the doors to Woodcock Smokery just outside the village of Skibbereen. It is here that Sally has prepared cold and hot smoked wild salmon, mackerel, kippers, tuna and haddock in a kiln over native hardwoods using no additives or dyes for decades.

Her commitment to exclusively smoking wild fish ran into an obstacle when the Irish government complied with an EU campaign to prohibit the extraction of wild salmon from the ocean fishery where the family sourced their salmon. It wouldn't do for the wife of a fisherman to smoke farmed fish, so Sally resigned herself to closing her business. But in an example of how paths in life frequently find their way back to their origins, Sally connected with a family in eastern Scotland who began supplying her with sea caught salmon once more.

" There are no strangers here,
only friends you have not met. **"**

WILLIAM BUTLER YEATS

Cork
TRAVEL GUIDE

For food lovers, a visit to West Cork, with its abundance of ardent food producers creating some of Ireland's most beloved and renowned artisan products, is essential. The picturesque town of Skibbereen is a good home from which to explore the region's abundance of weekend markets, food shops and producers crafting everything from cheese to smoked fish to organic beef.

West Cork Distillers is just outside of town and offers tastings of its small-batch spirits, including Drombeg whiskey, Two Trees vodka and Lough Hyne liqueur. Durrus Farmhouse Cheeses provides tastings of its raw milk cheeses along with a viewing window to learn about the process as it happens. Glenilen Farm welcomes visitors to learn about the challenges and rewards of running a family-owned dairy and at Brown Envelope Seeds, Ireland's only independent full-time seed-saver, Madeline McKeever, will introduce you to the vital importance of seed saving.

Learn about organic beef fabrication from William Walsh, a passionate craft butcher who provides butchery demonstrations in collaboration with Annie May's Restaurant. The village of Schull teems with pubs and restaurants proudly serving local ingredients. Hackett's Bar is one of the finest, with a rotating selection of smoked meat and artisan cheese from Gubbeen, which is located just down the road.